# ANCIENT AND MEDIEVAL POLITICAL THINKERS

## From Plato to Padua

# ANCIENT AND MEDIEVAL POLITICAL THINKERS
## From Plato to Padua

**Dr. P.B. Rathod**
M.A., Ph.D.
***Reader***
Dept. of Political Science
Gulbarga University
**GULBARGA**

Commonwealth

**Ancient and Medieval Political Thinkers**



First Published 2005

ISBN 81-311-0036-7

*Published by*:
**Ajay Verma**
**For Commonwealth Publishers**
4831/24, Prahlad Street,
Ansari Road, Darya Ganj,
New Delhi - 110002
Phones : 23272541, 23257835
Fax : 91-011-23257835
e-mail-campusbooks@hotmail.com

*Typesetting by*:
**Stylish Laser Typesetter**
Delhi - 110053

*Printed at*:
**Roshan Offset Printers**
Delhi

# Foreword

It gives me a great pleasure in writing foreword of Dr. P.B. Rathod who is a rare academician working in the Dept. of Political Science, Gulbarga University, Gulbarga. Dr. Rathod crucial book is entitled 'Ancient and Medieval Political Thinkers from Plato to Padua'. is worth reading. In the first and second chapter, the learned author has scientifically and deeply explained about the Ancient Greek Political Thinkers like Plato and Aristotle. In chapter third, the eminent scholar have been comprehensively studied about 'Roman Political Thinkers'. In chapter fourth, fifth, sixth and seventh the author is completely devoted his time in writing about the Medieval Political Thinkers and they are known as Secularists.

In total this book on the 'Ancient and Medieval Political Thinkers from Plato to Padua, is a very comprehensive and well-researched. The work is well documented and researched by appropriate support of notes and references. In the end of the book Dr. Rathod has given a list of bibliography.

I am sure that this book is a useful source of material for advanced study and learning. I wish the writer of this book all the success in the years to come.

**Dr. Mallappa Amaravati**
Retd. Professor of Political Science
Gulbarga University (Gulbarga)

# Preface

I have a great pleasure in placing 'The Ancient and Medieval Political Thinkers from Plato to Padua' in the hands of the students of B.A. and M.A. studying political science in various Indian Universities. The book is also useful for candidates appearing in Civil Services Examination.

This book is the result of my teaching experience for many years. There are many books on the subject. What is the reason or justification for writing this book? The students will judge for themselves. I am confident that the students whose welfare has been ever dear to my heart will extend a warm welcome to my book. I am indebted to great writers on the subject whose books I have consulted.

I take this rare opportunity to express my heart felt thanks to Shri Ajay Verma, Commonwealth Publishers, New Delhi, who has been constant source of inspiration to me to write this book and to publish the same.

I have no words to express my gratefulness to my wife Mrs. Vimala and daughters Kaveri, Priyanka, Premalata and sons Rajesh and Harish for their moral support encouragement, patience and sustenance in completing this work

**Dr. P.B. Rathod**

# CONTENTS

# 1

# Characteristics of Greek Thought

## 1. Intellectual Curiosity

The Greek mind delighted in speculation, investigation. Most educated Greeks absorbed and emitted philosophy like the air they breathed. The teaching was causal and conversational. Greek philosophy long back strengthened and enriched. They mediated all essential elements of philosophy, thought them through and through Plato and Aristotle are the disasters of political thought. Greek philosophy is a everybody's affair and not the private pasture of a few highly trained specialists. The philosopher is simply wise men who thinks more deeply and coherently than most of us are capable of philosophy is found in the poets and novelists. Political philosophy in the west was the invention of the Greeks. The Greek political thought is characterized by curiosity and quest. The Greeks had an insatiable curiosity and mending quest for knowledge and wisdom.[1]

## 2. Rational Approach

Closely allied with curiosity is the rational approach of the Greek political thought. The whole Greek view of life is coloured by it. Young in souls, the Greeks were old when it came to reasoning. Thus in Greek thought religion imperceptibly passes into philosophy. Religion transformed the facts both of nature and of society. Men was the bearer of divinity not apart from it. He could therefore live freely as to the nature of life. The Greek mind attained deliverence and of conscience. Sin was physically and immediately punishable, repentance was redundant. The citizen was bound with the state both physically and mentally. They participated in public offairs. The size of the city was very small. The body, mind and soul these are inter-related. Reason flows from gifts those who have it is a privileged class. The privileged class alone have reason and can be free, the rest are unfree. Lifeis virtue. Virtue is reason and there in lies the key to Greek Art. Art is the identification of the beautiful and the good. The inner must find a perfect reflection in the outer. Art is thus subjective, the artist alone counts. Subject is a matter of indifference. The excellence was aesthetic as well as ethical. Music vitally affects character. Music became the center of Greek education, poetry could be admitted in an ideal state. By music they meant melody, verse, and dance. Music is balance per excellence. Virtue is not prior to beauty nor beauty to virtue. They are if you like twins, two ways of viewing a single fact. The good and the beautiful were the one and the same thing. Drama is the high priest of society and the dramatic is the instructor of mankind. Comedy is a fun of life. It holds a mirror to it.[2]

### 3. Quest for Truth

They are in search of truth. Truth was dialogued through questions and answers type *i.e.* though dialectic. Ethics is based on the belief that the universe is one, it is rational. Greece is the intelligence of the world.

### 4. Primacy of Discussion

In order to find out the truth, the royal high way lies through debate and discussion. Through discussion truth comes out.

### 5. Interest in the World

Thus, seen, the center of interest of the Greeks was the world, this world of ours. The heart of world is of course, man. This is the running theme of the Greek thought in its entirely. This man, must be the man whose mind is governed by the reason. Socrates held the view that the noblest of all investigations is the state. Man is the crown of species. This is the pre-occupation of Plato and Aristotle.

### 6. Individualistic Elements

Greeks went on to construct a theory of individualism. The individual, that is, the best judge of his own interests. The state is the outcome of a contract, as Plato says in republic. Law is a necessary evil and so is the state. This is the crux of Greek individualism.

**7. Idealism**

The Greeks had a great regard for the convention.[3] Ten men Aristotle said are too few for a city, a hundred, thousand are too many. Citizenship meant not merely the payment of taxes and a vote, it also implied direct participation in the management of the state as a soldier, as a judge, as a legislator in person not through a deputy. He must be able to reach the center of the government. He must be able to speak and vote in person hence the limitations of numbers. The idea of representative government was completely alien to the Greek political thought. Society was a living entity. Participation in state affairs was a right as well as a sacred duty. The individual is a part of the society, which is the whole. The individual is as Plato says 'Microscope'. The state is macroscope. The dichotomy of the self regarding and the other regarding functions of the individual is incomprehensible to the Greek mind. There is no conflict between the two at any stage or level, there is no question of the individual being sacrificed to the whole. The two are organically related, so that the best individual is the best citizen. No individual can realise himself except through the state. Man is social animal more social than animalistic. It is natural for him to live in society. Outside the society the life of thc individual therefore be against the individual, inside the society he develops his best. He lives and ought to live in society.

**8. Concept of Law**

According to Greeks, law was the breath of state. The law givers were inspired by divine power, law therefore, was the manifestation of God. The outcome of pre-natal contract. Law means Nature or God. Law was light and just which means convention or old practice. And justice is that which is according to law. The law and justice are the two sides of the same coin. This certainly does not mean that all laws are just or that law connot be improved upon. It does not mean that law seekers to embody justice which has an objective and binding validity. They made the identification between law and justice in actual practice. The identification could be achieved in the Ideal Republic.

**9. The Greek Theory of Quality**

The distinction between the Greek and the barbarian artisan was not casual, it was natural and fundamental. The Greeks believed in equality within a class, equality which was proportional not arithmetical. Inequality of status or rank or office is the outcome of inequality of gifts and talents. According to Greek political theory equality by itself is not ideal thing. It is on the contrary, unnatural, impracticable as well as undesirable.[4]

**10. The Greek Political Institutions**

The constitution of Athens and Sparta moulded Greek political philosophy.

**Conclusion**

The Greek state primarily appears to be aristocratic, it had a pronounced military character. Trade and industry were regulated to the backwaters. The traders and the artisans were excluded from the training in gymnastics philosophy. The Greek political theory emanated from the facts of Greeks life. Property was held in distrust. The ideal of the Greek citizen involved a complete fusion of public and private life.

## Plato (427-347 B.C.)

Plato was born in 427 B.C. in Athens. He was born in a well-to-do aristocratic family. Thus he was born in Athens best of the Greek politics. He was born and brought up in aristocratic environments. Hence he had leanings towards aristocracy and was a great critic of democracy. From his mother's side, he was related to the great law-giver, Solon. From his father's side he belonged to a distinguished family. He was brought in luxury and comfort, he was handsome and vigorous youth. He had served in Army.

He had travelled widely and had gained a lot of wisdom and experience. He founded the academy in order to put into practice his ideas about education. Plato was the disciple of socrates, the noblest and wisest man of his times. The fact that the Athenian government sentenced his master to death shocked him much. In the closing of his years of life, were happy and he was amply satisfied with the work of his pupils. In fact, he never grew old and was always working, guiding and inspiring disciples. Plato died in 347 B.C. at the age of eighty.

## HIS WRITINGS

**1. The Republic : 386 B.C.**

His political philosophy is reflected in the Republic, Statesmen and the Laws. His aim is to established "Ideal State". The republic is the greatest of his treaties. It deals with inter-connected and inter linked subjects.[5] This book was written when he was 40 years. This publications consists of 10 books, out of which books 5, 7 are very important. They are concerned with the ideal state. Book I deals with justice. Book 2, 3, 4 deals with education. The republic is the most inspiring book of Plato. Thus, Plato wrote many books of which three are very famous—'The Republic,' 'The Laws' and 'The Statesmen'. The republic is the most inspiring of all these. In the republic we see a clear picture of Plato's political philosophy. Infect, the republic deals with many branches of human knowledge—Ethics, Psychology, Sociology etc. The republic has a wide range of subject matter and includes all branches of human knowledge is not without reasons. We may enumerate the following reasons why so many branches of human knowledge have been discussed in the Republic.

Different social sciences like Ethics, Economics, Psychology, Sociology and Politics were not so distinctly demarcated in Plato's days as they are today. All these sciences had man as their subject-matter and centred round the proposition, man is the measure of all things. The proper study of mankind is man. Life of the citizens in the city-state of Athens was not demarcated into different spheres as it is in the modern state. 'Polis' or the city-state embraced all aspects of the individuals life. For the Greek citizen, there was no separate religious life, no separate economic or social life. The city state was the end of his life. He got all opportunities for the development of all aspects of his personality. For this reason, Plato included all branches of human knowledge in the Republic. Since Plato wrote his great book in the form of a dialogue, it was possible for him to discuss various subjects, yet keeping to the central theme and maintaining the unity of the whole treatise. The method used by Plato gave him ample opportunity to enlarge the scope of the book.

Since man is the subject matter of the Republic, the great treatise is a single organic whole having unity inspite of variety and richness of themes and inspite of the diversity of those themes. Man's thoughts and actions in society have been fully discussed. The concepts of the idea/state and justice have been elaborated in a masterly and skilful manner. The philosophy of human life has been presented in a dramatized manner. The Republic is a drama on the complexities, varieties, intricacies, diversity and unity of human life.

The republic is a treatise on man. Therefore, the first question for Plato is who is a good man and how can a good man be made. To us, this question is a question of moral philosophy, but for Plato, moral philosophy was not separated from political philosophy. In Plato's view, a good man could exist only in a good state. Good individuals good state. There could not be good individuals in a bad state and there could not be a good state if the individuals were bad. The individual is 'The State in Little' The state is the individual 'Write Large'.[6]

From the question, who is a good individual there follows naturally another question, what is a good state. One question leads to the other and the republic becomes several treatises combined into one.

We may classify the subject matter of the republic in the following way :

*(a)* A treatise on metaphysics—Showing the unity of all things in the idea of the good.

*(b)* A treatise of moral philosophy—Dealing with the virtues of the human soul. The union of these virtues leads to the concept of justice.

*(c)* A treatise on education—According to Rousseau, "The Republic is not a work on politics, but a finest treatise on education that ever was written."

*(d)* A treatise on political science—Discussing properly, marriage, communism etc. in the ideal state.

*(e)* A treatise on philosophy of history—Explaining how changes take place in history and how the ideal states define into tyranny.

All these different subjects were parts of one general theme-man. Therefore, the above-mentioned treatises have been skillfully woven into one. The Republic is like a garden, having different portions for the different flowers and fruits. The garden is one. This is the garden of complex human nature and equally complex human society. The Republic is like a jewel box containing jewels, pearls and diamonds of various colours and sizes, but the box is one full of precious jewellery.

**2. The Statesmen : 360 B.C.**

It was written in 360 B.C. when he was 67 years. It deals with politics and the role of an individual in politics and discussed how the people should be governed. According to him, a true politician should try to educate the citizens and aim at promoting virtue and justice.

**3. The Laws : 347 B.C.**

It was written in 347 B.C. at the age of 80. Laws are necessary even for the guidance of the kings. Rulers should not kept above the laws. He has tried to be more practical in this book. Now he had begun to realize that the laws are necessary even for the guidance of the kings.

**Plato's Ideal State**

Plato depicted his ideal state in the republic. In other words, Plato portrays the ideal state in his Republic. State will be the true copy of the heavenly model. Whether the ideal state exists or not is not the point. The rulers should be those who understand the good and real, otherwise, "Ideal state cannot function". The point for the great philosopher is what the ideal state ought to be. State rests on the principle of necessity and utility. The state is supreme means to supreme good. Under the guidance of the philosopher king or the guardians will the state reach perfection, balance, and harmony. The first condition of the ideal state that the Plato argues is that it must be properly led. Proper leadership can give only those who have knowledge and wisdom. Ideal state must be governed by those who have virtue or wisdom. If wise rule the state, state becomes wise. Plato says no two men can said to be equal. Plato's ideal state is based on the principle "The right man in the light place," and best men in the highest place. It should not be understood to mean the privileged men in a privileged place.[7]

Plato says, political power, must be in the hands of those who know the art of state craft. Those alone who have been gifted and endowed by nature with the best intellectual faculties and who have acquired adequate education essential for an ideal ruler should rule. In the hands of such rulers happiness, prosperity, goodness and welfare of the people will prevail. The ignorant must be kept aside. In the hands of ignorant, the city state will be doomed. The rule by the ignorant means suffering, evil and maladies of all types. Plato says 'Virtue is knowledge and ignorance is vice'. The interests of the ruled suffer when the ignorant and incompetent rule. The 'ruled' are benefited when there is the rule of a few or one wise, gifted, specially trained individual. The philosopher rulers alone can free the individuals from such. The wise will be the rulers in the 'Ideal State'. The wise will be the bearers of excellence, knowledge and virtue.

Like a great psychologist, Plato believed in individual differences. Everybody is not fit to do every type of work.

Talents differ. Some are born to rule, others must follow. The man is said to be master of himself. The better part would rule over the worse. According to Plato, there are three parts in the soul, the appetitive, the spirited and the rational. There are three classes in society, corresponding to these three parts of the soul—the workers, the soldiers and the Philosophers. The ideal state is that in which justice prevails and justice will prevail in an ideal state where the workers work honestly, soldiers fight bravely and the philosophers rule wisely. Plato says that God put gold into the heads of the philosophers, silver into the heads of the soldiers and iron into the heads of the workers. Just as gold is more precious than silver and iron, similarly, philosophers are superior to the soldiers and the workers. The philosophers alone have the light to rule, because they are endowed with wisdom.

Ideal state should be governed by those who have virtue or wisdom. If wise rule the state, state becomes wise. If numerous class of fighters have courage, the whole society or state becomes courageous. The soldiers must be trained, instructed and educated in music and gymnastics. Uninstructed courage is that of a wild beast or that of a slave. Soldiers should lead a hand and simple life. Ideal state must be properly led and nourished.

The idea of classes and souls can be made clear with the help of the following diagram :

Individual — — — — — — — — — — — — — — — State
Rational self or reason ⟶ Philosopher-Rulers
Spirited self ⟶ Soldiers
Appetitive self ⟶ Workers

No individual is self-sufficient in society. We are dependent upon others for the satisfaction of our needs. For satisfactory satisfaction of these needs, there is exchange of services. Each individual should perform with complete devotion the function assigned to him. It is the duty of each individual to perform his own function in the most up light-manner, never trying to encroach upon those functions for which he is not fit by birth and education. The harmony and balance in the state will never be disturbed so long as men live upto the psychological principle of specialization of functions. A deviation from this principle will lead to disharmony and confusion.

An ideal state is that where there is justice the concept of justice is one of the most important theories in Plato's republic.[8] For Plato, justice is not legal concept as we think of it in modern times. Since there is specialization of functions, justice in the state prevails when workers work honestly, soldiers fight bravely and philosophers rule wisely. The producers correspond to an appetite, the fighters to spirit and the rulers to reason. Every class must function in co-ordination with each other and virtuously in its best form. The producers must act temperately, the fighters must operate courageously, the rulers must govern wisely. Thus seen, the virtue of producer's is temperence (as in case of appetite), the virtue of the fighters is courage (as in the case of spirit), the virtue of rulers is wisdom (as in the case of reason) and the virtue of society as a whole is justice (as in the case of mind as a whole). Society is thus mind writ large. Justice in society is a mere reflection of justice in mind. Justice is knowledge. Justice is the supreme virtue.[9]

But it is a process, it is an idea not an object. It is not phenomena. It can be perceived not by senses but by reason. It is the product of the reason. All production and institutions are the reflection of ideas. Everyone can perceive the supreme idea. Nature had not made everyone alike. Latent capacities and talents differ. Justice can be acquired by education.

Thus, Plato's theory of justice is comprehensive as it includes virtue, knowledge, integrity.[10] These can be attained positively by education and negatively by communism. Plato infact would prefer community living. Citizens can make the state just and not the state makes the citizen just. Once this is attained the ideal state is complete. Philosopher must rule the nation.

This is the sketch of the ideal or the perfect state. In an ideal state individual will be really free.

**Plato's Communism of Wives and Property**

For the philosophers and the guardians he advocated a kind of military monasticism. Where no separate family life is permitted, private property is forbidden. Simple life does not satisfy men who are by nature acquisitive, ambitions, competitive, and jealous.[11]

Leadership is placed by bossism, and statesmanship by politics. Leadership and statesmanship mean the co-ordination of social forces. Plato says that from 35 to 50 the select guardians would be compelled to hold any military office. Plato pleads that the marriages should be of such types that only good children were produced. Marriage was regarded by Plato as a means of producing healthy and efficient citizens. It could lead to healthy offspring's. The child was looked upon as a member of a family. The whole connexion between men and women to be regulated by the state. The children soon born are to be carried off to a common nursery, there to be reared together undistinguished by the mothers, who will suckle in differently any infant that might be assigned to them. But again, within the guardian class, there is equality of men and women. They are treated alike and they are intended and live together and have no private life of term own. It is often spoken of as communism of wives and property.[12]

The guardian's will have no wives. They are devoted not to a women but to the community. Friends should have all things in common including women and children. The girl are to have exactly the same education as boys learning music, gymnastics and the art of war along with the boys. Within the select class, women are to have complete equality with men in all respects. The education makes a women good guardian. If a women shows herself capable of public office, let her rule. If a man shows himself to be capable of washing dishes, let him fulfill the function which providence has assigned him.

The men and women must live in common houses and meet at the common meals. None of them will have specially anything his or her own, they will associate at gymnastic exercises to have intercourse with each other. Matrimony will be beneficial and therefore sacred. But marriages can be useful and beneficial only if they are eugenically sound.[13]

Plato then goes on to deal with the ripe age of producing good children a women from 20 to 40 and a men from 25 to 55. Anyone who violates these restrictions would be guilty of an unholy and unrighteous thing.

Once the length sort of children are born, the state will take charge of them because the parents should not know that they are the parents of a particular children. All children of guardian's shall be taken from their mother's at birth and brought up in common, their particular parentage will be lost in the scuffle. Inferior children's were deformed. The mother will have no getting up at night or other trouble, but will handover all this sort of thing to the nurses and attendants. This is the fantastic scheme of community of wives which Plato poetically drew up.[14]

**Community of Property**

The rulers and the guardians, Plato speaks will not have houses or lands or any other property. They will have no property expenses. They will have just sufficient and no more. Gold and silver are forbidden. But wealth and property are harmful and both are equally banished from his ideal Republic. They should not possess land, house, money, community of property and wives that makes them to think interms of "Mine and Thine."[15]

Plato wanted to abolish property in order to achieve unity, harmony and justice in the ideal state. He convinced that the mere abolition of property is not enough because the need, desire and greed of property continues as long as there is family. According to Plato, attachment to the family is the cause of weakness and many temptations for the individual. The individual wants to acquire more and more property because of his attachment to the family. Attachment to the family hinders a men from performing his duties honestly, efficiently and effectively. It is in the interest of the unity of the state that along with the institution of property, the institution of family should also be abolished for the guardians the soldiers and the philosopher rulers so that they may be free from the bondage of mine and thine and may perform their duties without prejudice and partiality.

Plato wants the guardians to be entirely unselfish in order to perform their duties successfully. For this reason, he suggests communism of property for them as greed for wealth leads to corruption and prevents him from the performance of duties honestly. At the same time Plato is convinced that attachment for the family results in the greed for wealth. He, therefore, suggested abolition of family for the guardians.

## FUNDAMENTAL PRINCIPLES OF COMMUNISM OF FAMILY

### 1. Applicable to the Guardians Only

Plato's communism is meant for guardians only—the soldiers or the fighters and the philosophers rulers, just as his communism of property is meant for these two classes only. Plato wants these two classes to be free from the need, desire and greed of property and from the bondage of permanent marriage and family system. The words 'mine' and 'thine' are not for the guardians.

### 2. Unity and Justice

Plato is of the opinion that communism of family is essential for unity, harmony and solidarity in the state. When the guardians are free from the temptation and greed of property, when they are not bound by the family ties, when the words mine and thine do not apply to wives and children, when there are common pleasures and pains, there will be unity, harmony and solidarity in the state.[16]

Similarly, there will be justice in the state when the ruling class is free from the desire of property and bondage of family. Justice prevails in the ideal state when the different classes perform their functions honestly. The guardians can do their duty in an honest manner only when they have no property and no family.[17]

### 3. A Novel Scheme

Communism of wives is a novel scheme. Like the rule of philosophy, this scheme is also an innovation of Plato. It is an original suggestion of Plato in this form, though he had some examples before him. For example, in Sparta, women were free to join the military along with men.

### 4. Emancipation of Athenian Women

Plato suggested communism of family to emancipate Athenian women. The condition of Athenian women was very miserable in Plato's times. In Plato's times the Athenian women were confined within the walls of the house. They were married at the age of 15 and passed from seclusion of one house to the other. They had no freedom to take part in public life. Their sphere was the home. Men had full control over public affairs. The Greek city was for most purposes a men's club.

## Reason's for Communism of Wives and Children

Plato supports communism of wives and children for many reasons :

### 1. Political Reason

Plato feels that private property will always encourage the greed for property and attachment to the family will hinder the guardians from the performance of their duties. According to Plato, loyalty to the family is a stumbling block in the way of loyalty to the state. When all the guardians feel that they are the members of the 'same family' and all the women and children belong to them in common, there will be no friction and no strife in the name of mine and thine. Plato says guardians are 'watch-dogs' are free from the bondage of private property.

According to Plato, the greatest good of the community will result from the abolition of private family system. Plato feels that under his system of common wives and children, there is no danger of any internal strife or rebellion and the state will be a place of perfect happiness and bliss.

**2. Eugenic Reason**

Plato suggests community of wives in order to improve the race. He feels that permanent marriage relationship of the monogamous type weakens the race. He suggests temporary marriages between the best couples under state control. The state will thus have the chance of getting the best children and there will be improvement of the race. Weak and deformed children are not needed in Plato's ideal state. He wants to regulate marriages to improve the race.

**3. Moral Reason**

Plato suggested the scheme of communism of wives because he was perturbed by the deplorable condition of women in Athens. Women are kept within the walls of the house before and after their marriage. They were considered to be fit for house hold duties alone. Their life was a drudgery. So, Plato wants, "Break the Walls." Let women breathe fresh air outside the homes. Let them take proper places in shouldering the responsibilities of the state affairs.[18]

According to Plato, men and women are equally talented and there is no difference in the sexes regarding their ability to perform public duties. The state suffers a loss if women who are in no way inferior to men and who constitute an important section of the population of the state are kept within the walls of the homes and are not given the opportunity of performing public duties along with men.

Plato also thinks that the principles of justice and morality demand that women should be liberated from bondage of household drudgery and should be participants in the performance of their duties as guardians.

**A Brief Description of Wives and Children**

We can have a very clear picture of Plato's communism of wives and children if we understand the following points :

**1. No Permanent Weddings**

Plato is a great enemy or opponent of the system of permanent weddings or marriages. He feels that permanent monogamous marriages result in the enslavement of women and hinder them from showing their talents to perform public duties.

**2. Living Together**

All guardians men and women are to live in common barracks. They will dine at the common tables. All the guardians are to live on the salaries paid in kind by the farmers, workers and artisans.

**3. Temporary Marriages**

Plato suggests temporary marriages between the best of men and the best of women for one year. The number of couples to be so united by temporary marriages will be fixed by the state keeping in view the number of children required by the state. These marriages will be performed at a particular nuptial season.

**4. Age-Limits for Marriage**

Plato is of opinion that women are to be married between the ages of 20 and 40 and men between the ages of 25 and 55. Whenever there is a violation of these age rules, the children born of such parents should be killed immediately.

**5. Separation of the Parents from Each Other After the Birth of the Child**

Plato suggests that after the birth of the child, the parents should be separated from each other and should wait to be united to other members of opposite sex at the proper time. It is however, essential that the male and the female should be in perfect health and should be within the prescribed age limits.

**6. Children to be Separated from the Mothers**

Children born as a result of these temporary marriages are to be separated from their mothers immediately after they see the light of the day. The children are not to know their parents and the parents are not to know their children. They are to be taught that they are common children of all the parents. Thus, there will be no single private family system. All the guardian class thus becomes one big family and there is no cause of jealousy, friction and disputes of any type. There will be a perfect unity, harmony and justice in the state.[19]

**7. Weak Children to be killed Immediately after their Birth**

One of the most important reasons for Plato's communism of wives and children is the improvement of the race. In his anxiety to have the best children for the ideal state, he suggests an extreme measure. He suggests that weak, deformed, disfigured and diseased children should be killed immediately after their birth. For the performance of their duties in the ideal state, mentally and physically healthy children are needed. There is no place for weak, diseased disfigured and deformed children in Plato's ideal state because such children are unfit to perform their duties.

**8. Children to be Brought up by the State**

Plato is very anxious to bring up children under state control, so he frees the mothers from the duty of bringing up children. He suggests that all the children born as a result of temporary marriages should be immediately separated from the mothers and should be brought up under state control. It is the duty of the state to make arrangements for state nurses. All these children are to receive education under strict state control.[20]

**Criticisms**

Plato has suggested his moral and original scheme of communism of wives and children with the object of improving the race emancipating the women and bringing about unity, harmony and justice in the ideal state. We sympathise with the aims. We appreciate and admire them. Yet we cannot agree with Plato's scheme of communism of wives and children. Inspite of the noblest aims and intentions of Plato, his scheme is full of several defects and cannot stand the test of communism.

We may note the following points of criticism against Plato's communism of wives and children.

### 1. Plato Ignores the Basic Difference Between Men and Women

In his anxiety to liberate from the drudgery of the household duties, Plato ignores the basic and natural differences between the two sexes. There are psychological and physical differences between men and women and in assigning them duties, we have to keep in view these differences.

Nature has endowed with certain qualities which enable them to perform certain types of duties which men cannot perform. Similarly, women cannot be expected to perform certain duties which men alone can perform. To think that men and women are equal in all respects is to challenge nature which has made them different. Of course, no sensible human being will like to keep women within the four walls of the home, but, to bring absolute equality between the two sexes is impossible. All this does not mean that women are inferior to men. It only means that in certain spheres of work, women alone are suitable and in certain other spheres men alone can perform the duties efficiently and effectively.[21]

### 2. Women is the Centre of the Family

By nature, women is the center of the family. She is the most suitable person to bring up the children. To separate children from the mother is against the principles of human psychology. This separation is intolerable both by the mother and the children.

Of all living creatures, human children need care and affection of the mother for a longer period. By depriving them of parental affection and protection, Plato is trying to take away all tenderness and sweetness from their life.

### 3. Relation Between Husband and Wife—A Permanent Spiritual Bond

Plato reduces men and women to the level of mere animals, by his arrangement of temporary marriages. To have children is only one of the aims of marriage. Plato thinks this is to be the only aim of marriage. The relation between husband and wife is a permanent friendly relation based on deep spiritualism. To bring men and women together for a short period by a system of temporary marriages merely for the purpose of having children and then to separate them is to cut the roots of the basic motivating force in life-love. By ignoring the noblest sentiment like love, Plato is forgetting the very meaning and purpose of life.

Marriage is a life long friendship based on the highest and the noblest foundation of love and Platonic philosophy is unjust to human race in this respect.

**4. Family is the Centre of Culture**

The institution of family is the unit of social life. It is the center of culture, recreation and education. It is the eternal school of social life. There can be no better teachers than the parents. There can be no better friends than the parents. There is nothing sweeter for the parents than the children. The children are the flowers, the family is the garden and the parents are the gardeners. Like flowers, the children can bloom only in a free atmosphere of the family and not in the rigid state controlled atmosphere as Plato suggests.[22]

Paternal instinct is not so wicked as Plato supposes. This instinct is the purest and the noblest and has motivated the noblest deeds. It is not true that loyalty to the family takes away our loyalty to the state. The real philosopher is a patriot-one who does not allow family attachments to stand in the way so far as his duties to the state are concerned. The real philosopher brings a harmony between the family and the state and leads a balanced and harmonious life. Greater good has been done to mankind by men and women who brought up their children with care and affection and still devoted themselves to the higher interests of the state than by those who had no families

**5. State-Control too Rigid**

Plato's scheme is so rigid, strict and stringent that the individual is reduced to the level of a mere means. He demands so much control and self-control which is intolerable for mortal and fallible human beings. It is not possible for human beings to subject themselves to the excessive control and self control that Plato demands. He takes away fall freedom from the life of the individual and freedom is very essence of life. The personality of the individual cannot be developed in a balanced and the harmonious way when there is so much state control.

**6. Too Logical**

Plato is expert in deductive reasoning. He starts with certain deductive principles and goes on drawing inferences from them logically. He is a successful logician, but ignores human feelings and sentiments altogether.

**7. Impracticable**

Plato's scheme of community of wives and children is only utopian. It is impracticable. It is only imaginary. Plato does not give the details of his scheme. He himself expresses a doubt about the possibility of the scheme being put into practice.

**8. Suggestion to Kill Weak, Deformed Children Cruel and Unjust**

Plato's suggestion that weak and deformed children should be killed is cruel and unjust. One of the functions of the state is to take care of the weak and sick.[23]

**Plato's Theory of Education**

Plato wants to construct an ideal state in which there is justice, specialization of functions, divisions of labour based on the principle of division of society into workers, soldiers and the philosopher-rulers. Justice in the 'Ideal State' prevails when the workers work honestly, soldiers fight bravely and the philosophers rule wisely. In order to find right type of philosopher-rulers, Plato suggests and negative method of communism of wives and property and also a positive method of a system of education. He attaches so much importance to education that some writers think that the Republic is more a treatise on education than on politics.

Plato's theory of education was logically derived from the following sources.

**Socratic Dictum-Virtue is Knowledge**

Plato's theory of education is logically derived from Socratic dictum-virtue is knowledge.[24] Plato was greatly influenced by the Socratic dictum or maxim-virtue is knowledge. From this dictum he came to the conclusion that only those who know will rule. There can be no virtue without knowledge. How can we do good unless we know what is good. Virtue can be known and virtue can be taught. If virtue can be taught, there must be an educational system to teach it.

Education is the foundation on which the walls of justice are built and on which the mighty structure of the ideal state stands. Plato's theory of education is the road to the ideal state. According to Plato, the most important duty of the state is to give education to its citizens. Plato's says, "The state is first and foremost an educational institution. If the state neglects education, it matters little what else the state does."

According to Plato, there are two aspects of education-individual and social. The inward reality and truth can be seen by the individual with the eyes of soul. It is also a social process. The process of education results in the creation of social consciousness in the individuals and they are enabled to adjust themselves to society. They are equipped with proper knowledge and training to perform their duties according to their station in society. Education is good for the individual and for society. It is good in itself. It enables us to contemplate the reality. This reality is behind all time and existence. Plato says that we should do our duty towards our fellows even when we are in contemplation. In Plato's educational system, we find a mixture of Athenian and Spartian systems of education with additions of his own ideas. Plato's educational system is a combination of the Spartan system and the Athenian system with an addition of Plato's idealistic ideas.[25]

**Features of Plato's Educational System**

We may enumerate some of the most important features of Plato's educational system.

**1. Education is State-Controlled**

Since education is of such supreme importance for moulding the characters of the citizens, for enabling them to perform their functions to secure justice in the ideal state, Plato does not want to leave it to private hands for in case it is left in private hands, there is danger of its being commercialized as a source of making money and the real aim of education may not be realized. For Plato, the state is one supreme agency of education. The state alone can impart the right type of education suited to the individual. No private agency should be allowed to undertake a task of such an important, significant and vital type.

Plato does not exclude women from the scheme of education. He does not see any difference between men and women about their capacity and right to education. Since both men and women are to work for the ideal state, both are entitled to the same type of education. Plato wants to free women from the routines of family life so that they may be eligible for the same offices as men.[26]

**2. Not Clear About Peasants and Artisans**

Plato does not give his views clearly and definitely about the type of training and education to be imparted to the artisans and peasants. Plato sketches an elaborate plan for the education of the philosopher rulers. He also talks of the education of the gifted and promising children of the peasants and artisans.

**3. Strict Censorship on All Works of Literature and Art**

Plato places a strict censorship on all works of literature and art. He wants to take precautions against all those works of art and literature which may have unhealthy, adverse and immoral effects on the minds of the young. Plato wants to save the young from bad moral influences. The decision what literature is good or bad for the youth is to be left ultimately to the rulers. He wants to expunge all passages which weaken the courage of the youth.

### 4. Compulsory Education

Since education is state-controlled, the necessary conclusion is that it is compulsory. Plato gives no option to the parents in this matter of supreme importance. He does not want to leave it to the sweet will of the parents to educate or not to educate the children. All children have to be educated according to a set scheme. Thus, it is clear that Plato is a fore-runner of all those thinkers who believe that education of all the citizens is a necessary condition for healthy development of individual and the state. Illiteracy is a great curse.[27]

### 5. Education Leads to the Ideal State

Education for Plato is so important that he makes the ideal state the product of education. In Plato's ideal state the philosophers rule. There can be no philosopher rulers if there is no education. The philosophers become philosophers after a systematic and disciplined education. Take away education and there are no philosopher rulers, no justice and no ideal state.

The entire structure of the ideal state with philosopher rulers guiding, ruling and administering justice falls to pieces if there is no education. Thus, education is the strongest foundation for the total structure of the ideal state where the philosophers rule and justice prevails. The edifice cannot be constructed without foundation. The philosopher of the academy is far-sighted enough to see that the welfare, prosperity, happiness and harmony for the individuals and the state are dependent upon education. He was predicting the role of education in the life of the individual and in creating good government.[28]

### 6. Training of Philosopher-Rulers

Plato starts with the first principle that virtue is knowledge and therefore, it can be taught and should be taught. Education should be so planned that the right type of rulers are trained. These are the philosopher rulers who alone can free the city states and the human race from the evils, ills, maladies and maladjustments.

**7. Education Good for the Soul**

Plato attaches great importance to the spiritual aspect of education. Just as the body needs food for its development, similarly the soul needs food.

**8. Education is for Life-Time**

Education according to Plato is not limited to a particular period in the individual's life. It is a continuous process. As long as the individual lives, he realizes education. The content of education varies for different age-groups. The philosopher rulers receive education upto the age of 35 and even continue to receive it upto the age of 50.

**Phases and Programmes of Education**

The key note of Plato's philosophy is the construction of the ideal state. The gymnastics is directed towards the welfare of the soul as well as of the body. Education includes arithmetic, geometry, astronomy, harmonies and dialectics.

The guardians must be trained in truthfulness. Education must be liberal. Those who learn the education must be bold, courageous and fearless. He must be gentle and not rude and unsocial. He must have real pleasure in learning. The objectives of education, therefore, will be the cultivation of quick intelligence, memory, sagacity, statesmanship, truthfulness, gravity, decorum and courage.[29]

Education begins even before birth. Education thus, begin before birth. Therefore, no men and women shall procreate unless in perfect health. Then the children of guardians shall be taken from their mothers at birth and brought up under a close state supervision. For the first 10 years education will be prominently physical and play and sports would be the entire curriculum. The unhealthy ones may be allowed to perish. Music imparts harmony and conducive to health. It moulds character. Music refines emotions and preserves health. It even curses diseases of the mind. It affects the springs of thought and action. Music will taught from 10 to 16 years after which individual would stop though communal songs would go on.

Even mathematics, history, and science can be taught through verses and songs. Bodily exercise, when compulsory does not harm to the body. He said children must be made hardy and taken to see the battle on horse back. Plato also believed in the immortality of the soul and transmigration and rebirth.[30]

At the age of 20, there will be a test which will result in great weeding out. The test will be three fold-labours, lessons and dangers. The stupid, cowardly will be eliminated. The test will be severe, impartial and objective. Those who pass will receive a further training of 10 years up to the age of 30. At 30, there will be another test. Those who quality will be elevated to the higher honour. Those who are wedded out will join the ranks of the warriors or executive aides or military officers. God has so willed gold, brass, iron. Only few are made gold and they alone will be the guardians.[31]

From 30 to 35 years, philosophy will be taught, which means to think clearly, to rule wisely. They will study the doctrine of ideas and forms which we have already examined. Metaphysics holds or occupies a central place in the scheme of education. At the same time, training in statesmanship would continue. The statesmen is he who runs the state efficiently, wisely and virtuously. The ruler must rule with or without the approval of the rule. As the good physician curses the patients with or without his approval.

At the age of 35, the philosopher would be put in the workshop of experience. They hold the military or other office which young men are qualified to hold. In this way, they will get their experience of life, they will stand form or flinch. This will go upto the age of 50. At the age of 50, they are to become the guardians.[31]

**Plato's Theory of Justice**

The central theme in Plato's republic is justice. He attaches great importance to justice in his book the republic. To us Justice suggests a legal meaning. But for Plato justice was a moral concept. Plato dismissed the definitions of justice as propounded by Thrasymachus, Cephalus and Glaucon. He said justice is an idea, an attribute of mind. It is easier to read a book in larger type than smaller, it is easier, therefore, to analyse justice on a larger scale than on the smaller scale of individual behaviour. He defines justice like this in his IV book justice is having and doing what is one's own. That means one should do his own business and should not interfere in the business of the others. If he interferes that is called as injustice. To Plato there are three springs of human behaviour—1. Desire—It includes appetite, impulse and instinct, 2. Emotion—Covers spirit, ambition and courage, 3. Knowledge—Implies thought, intellect and reason.[32]

Plato argues that although every man has three springs, but not in equal degrees. Every one do their own job-rulers to rule or govern, fighters would defend and protect, but not rule, the workers to produce. Thus, the producer is at his best in the economic field the warrior is at his best in battle, but they are both at their worst in public life. Only philosopher king is fit to guide the nation. Justice means balance and harmony. True knowledge is the knowledge of beauty and God. The beauty of the body is however, is nothing but the beauty of the soul. The rulers are philosophers and there are to be no innovations. His concern is to avoid change.[33]

In order to understand Plato's conception of justice, it is necessary to understand the following points.

### 1. Analogy Between the Individual and the State

The nature of the state is organic. The individual is the state in little. The state is the individual writ large. The individual is the smaller letter. The state is the large letter. It is easier to read the large letter than it is to read the small letter, but if we can read the large letter, we can also read the small letter. Justice exists not only in the state but also in the individual. In the state, it is bigger and more visible.

### 2. Close Relation Between the Individual and the State

The individual and the state, according to Plato one so closely related that in order to study the nature and character of one we have to study the nature and character of the other. In order to study the characters of men, we must study their states.[34]

**3. Origin and the Necessity of the State-Reciprocal Needs and Division of Labour**

According to Plato, the state arises from the fact that men here needs to satisfy. For the satisfaction of their needs, men depend upon others. No man is self sufficient. They take helpers and exchange services.

**4. Specialisation of Functions Division of Labour**

From the principle of exchange of services, there follows another important principle. This is the principle of specialization of functions and division of labour. Necessity of satisfaction of needs demands that there should be specialization of functions. All people do not have the same aptitudes. Aptitudes differ in different individuals. All men cannot do the same work effectively and efficiently. Some men do some work better than the others. If people do the work for which they have aptitude, they will acquire more and more skill in it.[35]

**5. The Role of the Philosopher-Ruler on the Basis of this Principle**

The philosopher-ruler has the knowledge to divide men according to their aptitudes for production of commodity for the satisfaction of human needs. The knowledge of the philosopher king gives him the right to rule. It also means his duty to rule wisely. Justice will prevail when there is specialization of functions and division of labour according to the aptitudes of the individuals as decided by the expert wisdom of the philosopher ruler.

**6. Classes and Souls**

The individual and the state are similar. If we know what is good for the individual, we also know what is good for the state. There is no conflict between the interests of the individual and those of society. According to Plato, the problems of the good state and those of the good individual are two sides of the same question. If one problem is solved, the other is automatically solved. The individual and the state are inseparable.[36]

Plato derives his conception of justice from his knowledge of human psychology. According to him, the human soul has three parts. The lowest part is the appetitive self. Higher than this is the spirited self. The highest self is the rational self or reason. A good or just individual is one in whom the rational self controls and guides the other two selves. Corresponding to these three selves, there are three classes in society. Corresponding to the appetitive self, there is the class of workers. Corresponding to the spirited self, there is the class of soldiers. Corresponding to the rational self, there is the class of philosopher rulers. Just as a good individual or a just individual is one in whom reason guides and controls the other two selves, similarly, a good state or a just state is that in which the philosophers rule. Justice will prevail in the state where the workers work honestly, soldiers fight bravely and philosophers rule wisely.[37]

**Three Principles in the Plato's Theory of Justice**

There are three principles in Plato's theory of justice :

1. **Non-interference.** This principle means that each class will do only that work which has been assigned to it on the basis of aptitude and will not interfere in the work of the other class.

2. **Specialization of Functions.** Everybody is not fit to do every type of work. Each individual can do and should do only that work for which nature has made him fit according to his aptitude and which society has assigned him.

3. **Harmony.** This means that there will be perfectly balanced and harmonious relations between individuals and individuals, between individual and classes, and between classes and classes and above all between the individuals, classes and the state. Justice harmonises the virtues of wisdom, courage and temperance which are the virtues of the three classes.[38]

**Criticisms**

There are many objections and criticisms to Plato's theory of justice.

**1. Too Moral.** The first weak point in Plato's theory of justice is that he insists on the moral aspect of human relations only. He has tried to reduce human beings to mere moral entities in society, forgetting all the time the imperfect side of human nature. There is no perfect individual and no perfect society. Hence, harmony is only imaginary.[39]

The conflicts between the individuals and individuals, between the individual and the class and between one class and the other are bound to arise. What is the remedy in platonic conception of justice? Can there be justice unless there is a legal sanction behind it and unless there is a power to enforce it. Judged by the standards of modern state and modern political science, Plato's conception of justice is too idealistic, too unrealistic and can never be realized.

**2. Total Population cannot be Classified.** Plato's classification of all the individuals in a state into three classes is arbitrary and artificial. The modern state has too large a population to be classified into three classes.[40]

**3. Too Artificial.** In his zeal to criticize democracy, Plato ignores thc principle of equality which is the basis of all social justice today. To divide human society into water-tight compartments is to try to arrange them into artificial groups. Though we cannot deny the existence of individual differences, yet we cannot make individual differences on the basis of the rule of philosophers.

**4. Too Orthodox and Makes Society Static.** Plato's principle of justice, based on specialization of functions and division of society into classes is too orthodox and makes society static and not dynamic. Can a worker improve his status in Plato's scheme of division of society into three classes? Plato favoured the rule by intellectual aristocrats. This is injustice to the majority of the people who must be ruled by these philosopher kings.[41]

**5. Soul cannot be Divided into Three Parts.** Human nature is an organic whole. Modern psychology does not divide human nature into three separate and water-tight compartments.

**6. Incomplete Development of the Individual.** Plato's theory of justice fails to bring about complete and harmonious development of the individual. In philosophers, virtue of wisdom is developed, what about the virtue of courage in them? In the soldiers the virtue of courage is developed, what about the virtue of wisdom in them? In the workers, only the appetitive self is emphasized. Thus, Plato's theory of justice leaves the individuals incompletely developed.[42]

**7. Dictatorship of the Philosopher-**Rulers. Plato's gives absolute power to the philosopher rulers. Concentration of power in the hands of one individual or a group of individual leads to corruption, however, well-educated and morally trained those individuals may be. Philosophers are fallible, mortals and are subject to temptations and corruption.[43]

**8. Plato's Theory Based on the Principle of Inequality.** Plato's theory encourages class domination. He believes that human beings are unequal. Modern society is trying to move more and more towards equality. Equality means justice. Inequality and special privilege mean injustice.[44]

## Conclusion

To sum up, we may say that Plato's conception of justice is moral and metaphysical and is far from being legal and therefore not applicable in modern state. Inspite of all the shortcomings and lacuna in Plato's theory of justice we cannot forget out indebtedness to this great philosopher foreshowing the light of virtue, goodness, harmony and justice. He has became the forerunner of subsequent political thinkers. Even his critics admire him for the loftiness of his thoughts.[45]

## REFERENCES

1. It is said that curiosity is the mother of knowledge and invention and Greeks successfully applied it to the different problems faced by the Greek city states.

2. Drama, Comedy and tragedy are the friends of life.
3. Customs, traditions and conventions are the base of Greek political philosophy.
4. Greeks said that talents differ and one should do his work according to his aptitudes, gifts, talents and capacities.
5. Sabine, A History of Political Theory, p. 39.

   'The Republic is mainly a treatise of ethics, individual and social.'
6. Barker, Greek Political Theory, p. 173.
7. Barker, *op. cit.*, pp.278-279.
8. Sabine, A History of Political Theory, p. 54.

   Sabine says, Justice is the bond which holds a society together.
9. Barker, Greek Political Theory, p. 177.

   Justice is nothing more and nothing less than man's performance of the part of which the purposes of society demand that he shall play.
10. Plato's Republic and Sabine, A History of Political Thought, p. 54.
11. Foster, Masters of Political Thought VI, p. 5.
12. Dunning, A History of Political Theories, p. 31.
13. Quoted by Foster in Masters of Political Thought, p. 84-85.
14. Plato's Republic.
15. Foster, Master of Political Thought, p. 90.
16. Barker, Greek Political Theory, p. 255.
17. Sabine, A History of Political Thought, p. 58.
18. Barker, *op. cit.*, p. 261.
19. Quoted by Foster, Masters of Political Thought, p. 86.

    "Men and women of like natures must live in common houses and meet at common meals. None of them will have specially any thing his or her own. They will be together and will be brought up together and will associate at gymnastic exercises."

20. Plato, Masters of Political Thought, p. 86
21. Quoted by Foster, *op. cit.*, p. 85.
22. Plato's Statesman.
23. Sabine, *op. cit.*, p. 98.
24. Dunning, History of Political Theory, p. 31.

    "In education, Plato sees the only true way to the permanent stability of the state."
25. Sabine, A History of Political Theory, p. 59.

    Sabine says, "Education is the positive means by which the ruler can shape human nature in the right direction to produce a harmonious state."
26. Gettel, History of Political Thought, p. 56.

    He says, "Certainly Plato places the fullest possible emphasis on education".
27. Rousseau says that the 'Republic' is the greatest treatise on education ever written.
28. Plato, Greek Political Theory.

    "Education is the vision of absolute truth and that vision is a vision of the individual soul."
29. Barker, Greek Political Theory, p. 216.

    "The soul can no more live without food for its activities than can the body, and therefore, so long as the soul lives, there is need of education to supply its nutriment."
30. Barker, *op. cit.*, p. 216.

    "Education is a matter of life-time. It is not only occupied with youth, it is also busy with maturity."
31. Dunning, *op. cit.*, pp. 30-31.
32. Sabine, A History of Political Thought, p. 54.

    "Justice is a bond which holds a society together".
33. Foster, Masters of Political Thought VI, p. 45.
34. Quoted by Foster from the Republic-Masters of Political Thought VI, p. 47.

35. Sabine, A History of Political Theory, pp. 48-49.

    "Society is to be conceived as a system of services in which every member both gives and receives."

36. Quoted from the Republic by Dunning, p. 33.
37. Gettel, History of Political Thought, p. 55.
38. Quoted from Plato's laws by dunning—A History of Political Theories, p. 38 foot note.
39. Barker, Greek Political Theory, pp. 344-345.
40. Barker, *op. cit.,* pp. 348-50.
41. Barker says, "Plato shows that the statesman is superior to the orator, the general and the judge statesmanship is supreme over all the other sciences concerned with action. The statesman's knowledge like himself is kingly."
42. Plato says, Justice in the ideal state prevails when the philosophers rule wisely, soldiers fight bravely and the workers work honestly.
43. According to Plato, God put gold into the heads of the philosophers, silver into the heads of the soldiers or fighters and iron into the heads of the workers. A gold is superior to the other two metals, similarly, philosophers are superior to the other two classes and have a right to rule
44. Plato says and came to the conclusion that the philosophers alone have the light to rule, since they have knowledge of what is good. Since 'virtue is knowledge', it follows that ignorance is vice. Only the philosophers have knowledge and wisdom. Therefore, they alone should rule. The many are ignorant, therefore, they must be ruled.
45. Plato says, attachment to the family is the cause of temptations. For the sake of the family, people try to acquire wealth even by unfair means. Therefore, Plato suggests abolition of the marriages and private families for the guardians.

# 2

# Aristotle

## (384-422 B.C.)

### His Life

In the history of political philosophy, Aristotle occupies a very position. According to Sir Fredrich Pollock, every student of political science should start his study of the subject after paying homage to Aristotle the father of political science.[1] European political thought is indebted to him to a very great extent. He is the originator of many terms, definitions and methods.

He was the ablest and the most famous of Plato's disciples was born at Stagira in a family connected with learning, medicine and the court. His father was a court physician. His childhood passed in the odour of medicine which is different from the scent of sanctity. From the start of his life, he developed an analytical and scientific bent of mind. Aristotle had a lust of wander, he was extravagant. He came into contact with Plato at the age of 30. He became the pride and soul of the academy and Plato began to call him as the intellect of his school, an intelligence personified. He was a lover of books. Plato called him a "Book Worm".

He undertake education under Alexander as his tutor, and buildup a tremendous reputation for scholarship and erudition. Aristotle, eloquent, learned, knowledgeable, acute, mentally sharp and intellectually profound. Alexander held Aristotle in great veneration and affection. Life is the gift of nature, but beautiful living is the gift of wisdom. He observed the characteristics and studied of birds, beasts, and fishes. Alexander was always impartial of schooling. The study of biology was a favourite to Aristotle. He also studied Zoology and Botanical material and made them experiment.[2] He was inspirer to scholars, philosopher, logicians, statesmen, orators, dramatists, poets etc.

## INFLUENCES ON ARISTOTLE

**Introduction**

All great men are influenced by the circumstances of their times and by writings and thoughts of other great men. Their surroundings, personal experiences and contact with other great people mould their philosophy. The question arises what factors influenced Aristotle's mind and moulded his political philosophy.[3]

It is of fundamental importance to know that Aristotle was influenced by the environment of his birth place Stagira, by his personal experiences, by his association with Alexander great as his tutor, and above all, by his association with Plato as his discipline.

We may note some of the important influences on Aristotle as follows :

**1. Influence of his birth place**—Stagira Aristotle was born in Stagira, a coastal state, situated at the Macedonian Coast. He remained there till the age of 17. It was natural that his young mind was influenced by the culture and conditions and environment of his birth place. At Stagira, Aristotle learnt that investigations in order to yield good results must be scientific. He studied the problems like a realist and not an idealist. With a realistic approach, he studied the constitutions of 158 Greek city states. Of course, the constitution of Athens still survives as an example.

**2. Influence of his father**—His father's influence on Aristotle was profound. His father was a physician in the court. From his father, Aristotle inherited an interest in biology. For this reason, his works show a deep interest in biological studies. It is because of this interest in biology that he compares the state with organism and the individual with organ.

**3. Influence of the conditions in the Greek city-states at that time**—Aristotle lived at a time when trouble and disturbance were shattering the peaceful conditions in most of the Greek city-states. In many of the Greek city-states, there was either democracy without law, or oligarchy with selfish rulers in power. There was so much turmoil in the Greek city-states that a thinker could not help thinking about the causes of all this turmoil and trouble. These conditions influenced Aristotle so much that he began to think about the actual happenings and the actual institutions rather than the ideas and the ideals.

**4. Influence of Plato**—Aristotle was a student in Plato's academy for a period of about 20 years. He joined the academy at the age of 17 and remained there for nearly two decades. Plato's academy attracted him because it was the best center for advanced studies.[4]

Plato's influence on Aristotle is apparent in the following points :

**I.** Man is a social Animal. Aristotle believes that man is a social animal. He says, "The man who can live alone is either a beast or a God. The idea about the social nature of man was learnt by Aristotle from Plato. He also learnt from him that the state is the result of needs of man.

II. The state is a moral institution. Aristotle borrowed from Plato the idea that the state is not only a political entity, but a moral and social institution and exists for the welfare and moral perfection of man.

III. Good life possible only in a small city-state. Plato had limited the population of the city-state to 5040. Aristotle said that the territory of the state was too large if one side of it was not visible from the other. Thus it is clear that both the philosophers believe that smallness of the state is necessary for good life.

IV. Only a few very capable, competent, well-trained and well-educated people have the right to rule. Both philosophers believed that government is not everybody's affair. The right to rule should be limited to well-trained and highly competent people. Everybody is not competent to rule.

V. Democracy is not the ideal form of government. Both the philosophers are critics of democracy. Plato says that it is the worst form of government. Aristotle also gives democracy the lowest place in his classification of governments. The vice of democracy is that it is the rule of the incompetent and the ignorant.

VI. Role of education in the state. Plato believed that the primary function of the state is education. The state should promote the virtues of the individual by the process of education. Plato's republic has been regarded the greatest treatise on education. Aristotle also believes that education is of utmost importance for the individuals. Education alone can bring about a healthy and balanced state. Right education alone can free them from the corrupt influences.

VII. Mixed State. In the Statesman and the Laws, Plato suggests that a mixed state—a combination of monarchy and democracy is most suitable for the interests of the people. Aristotle borrows the idea of the mixed state from his master Plato.

VIII. Very close relation between the individual and the state. Plato believed that there is a very close relation between the individual and the state. The individual is the state in little. The state is the individual writ large. The virtues of the state and the virtues of the individual are identical. Aristotle borrowed this idea from Plato.

**5. Influence of Greek Ideas**—Aristotle was strongly influenced by Greek ideas. We can trace the following Greek influences in his philosophy.

I. Greek superior to others. Like all Greeks of those days, Aristotle believed that the Greeks were superior to other nations. The Greeks and the Greeks alone were custodians of culture and philosophy.

II. Belief in the city-state. Aristotle believed like all Greeks that the city-state was the best political unit. He thought that the state was too large if one side of it was not visible from the other.

III. The city-state an end in itself. The city state embraced all the aspects of the personality of the Greeks. Aristotle thought that the large states were not so useful for human civilization as the small city-states. There could be no better life than the life in the city-state. The city-state was an end in itself.

IV. Whole greater and superior to the parts. A Typical Greek element in Aristotle's philosophy is that whole is prior to superior to, greater and better than parts. The individuals are the parts and society is the whole. For the sake of the whole, parts can be sacrified. For the sake of society, the individuals can be sacrificed.[5]

V. Citizenship—The characteristic of a free man. Another typical Greek feature of Aristotle's political philosophy was that citizenship was a special feature of a free man. For the Greeks citizenship actual participation in the affairs of the government. A slave was not a citizen, but a free man was a citizen.

VI. Justification of slavery. Aristotle's justification of slavery is typically Greek. He believed that slavery was justified by nature. He believed that the slavery were intellectually inferior. It is natural, therefore, that some men are masters and others are slaves. Aristotle thought that slavery is justified because it is useful.

**6. Aristotle's Association with Alexander the Great as a Tutor.** Aristotle was Alexander's tutor for 6 years from 342 B.C. till 334 B.C. Alexander's army conquered Persia and marched upto the Beas in India. He wanted to be a world conqueror. He conquests open a new chapter in the history of the world.

**7. Happy and Successful Life.** Aristotle's personal experience about family and property was very pleasant. He led a happy and successful married life. For this reason, he justified the institution of family and criticised Plato's communism of wives. He led a comfortable life. He had house, lands and servants. Therefore, he justified the institution of property. Aristotle's happy and comfortable life partly accounts for the difference in his views and those of Plato about family and property.

## Works of Aristotle

His works are in the form of lectures to the students. He was technical interms of formulas. His works are careful. He was into passionate or in any profound sense religious. He followed scientific method on Metaphysics. Whatever he touched he illuminated. He used logic method in his political works. He also used logic. He said animal, man, book, tree are universals. But universal are subjective notions, not objective realities. They are names and not things. He was interested in things. There is nothing common or general in man. There is man and in him he was interested.

He wrote Zoology and founder of Botany. He applied the general conclusions of his study of science and biology to politics. His theory of political cycles is based on his study of physics and meterecology. Environment affects human habits which determine social institutions. He studied Metaphysics. It is a primary philosophy he calls it, which lies beyond natural philosophy (physics). It deals with the science of being reality or existence. Aristotle formed reality in four categories. 1. The matter, 2. The external principles of motion, 3. The form, 4. The aim and end of the process. Thus, there is a material an efficient, a formal and a final course of everything.

## Theory of Good Life and Happiness

Aristotle's ethics is of primary importance to all students of political thought. It is a treatise. Everything we do is for the sake of goodness *i.e.* this in medicine, in health, in war victory, in house, in house building. This is the end and everything else is subordinated to achieve this end. Happiness is the final end of human aspiration and efforts. We choose happiness for our own sake and for no other purpose. Of course, there are ends which are not final such as pleasure, honour, intellect, wealth etc. These are subordinated aims directed towards happiness. But if happiness is the object of life, what is happiness? His answer is that good is to be found not in externals like wealth honour as most people imagine. Happiness is achieved through reason. Intellectual virtue is the most appropriate happiness. He says happiness is not a state, but an activity.[6]

What is virtue? He said great moral virtues courage, justice, temperence, gentleness, liberality etc. The right way is more efficient. Poverty is the curse and it must be removed. Property is good because it gives you freedom from care and worries. Friendship is the another external aid of happiness, because it is multiplied in sharing with him. A friend says Aristotle "is one soul in two bodies." But there can be only few friends and it he who has many friends has no friend. Fine friendship requires duration and implies stability of character.

Happiness is an object of action, is also a value. Every art, every science, every action, every moral choice involves an aim —the chief good. So politicians must have an aim. He also includes religion in it. This aim is happiness. In this sense, happiness is empirically based. It is the highest good. It desire in itself. It is the ultimate value. It is not instrumental but intrinsic. It means honour, pleasure or intellect. The true source of happiness is man's rational and social instinct or quality. Happiness is an activity, and man does not act when he dead. Happiness does not come in or after death. It comes in life. It is life. No man can be happy without external aids. External goods, freedom from want, good birth, good children, a beautiful wife, and no man can be happy if he lacks these. The community provide necessary conditions for the life of themind—property, family, friend. The community must be well ordered in the sense, that the extremes must be avoided. It must have a broad middle classmen who are neither rich nor poor, but solid sound citizens.

**Politics**

Politics is his master piece. It is a treatise. Politics is a Guide to constitution makers. According to some writers, Aristotle's politics is a practical handbook. Aristotle gives rules for the legislators in book IV, V and VI and discusses the nature of the existing states. The politics is a guide to the constitution makers. In this part of the politics which is concerned with actualities, Aristotle does not talk about the ethical purpose of the state. Even the worst ruler, the tyrant is told how best be can control the people. The politics is a great book on political science. It is really a light-house for all students of political science. It is a guide for the statesmen, legislators, administrations and the constitution makers. The politics is the most important of all the books written by Aristotle. It has been called the richest treasure that has come down to us from antiquity. It is thought to be a guide to the constitution makers—a great treatise on the science and art of government. The politics is a handbook for the statesmen and shows practical wisdom. Aristotle is the writer of this great treatise. The 'politics' is an incomplete and unfinished work. Eight books of the 'politics' are not properly arranged. In the politics, Aristotle makes the scope of political science wider. The politics is a practical handbook.[7]

Aristotle declares 'mixed constitution' as the best that is golden mean per excellence. Inductive reasoning he applies to the cycle of states. The Greek states provides a historical and institutional basis in politics. The politics is derived from 'polis'—it signifies a civic republic. It is a place of residence. To Aristotle, justice meant both ethical as well as legal, a moral value, as well as a legal quality. Similarly to him, Aristocracy meant the rule of the best, not the rule of the high born. Democracy the rule of the poor, not the rule of the all citizens. He said 'Man is a political animal. They are inclined to live in well-organised communities. He said, animals have souls, and plants do not have it. Polis is the state. Happiness is the goal of polis. Polis is a perfected community. Slavery is advantageous both a slave and a master. Women is to a men what slavery is to a master.

## ORIGIN, NATURE AND END OF THE STATE

### Introduction

Aristotle was a realist. Plato is a deductive thinker and proceeds from universals to particulars. Aristotle is an inductive thinker and proceed from particulars to universals. Plato starts with the principles, Aristotle with the facts. Aristotle gives fundamental characteristics of the state in the first book of the 'politics'. According to Aristotle, the state is the highest form of human association.[8]

Like Plato, Aristotle is a great critic of the sophists. He does not agree with the sophists that the state is artificial and is the result of conventions and contract. According to Aristotle, the state is a natural institution. Thus, the state is natural. Man is both rational as well as irrational. Happiness is achieved only in the state. Society and state are identical. He does not distinguish society from the state. The best individual is also a best citizen. The two ideals are indistinguishable and are mutually complementary. In it individual attain his ideal. It is the final form which man could attain. The state is whole. The individual is part. State is prior to individual. It is not based on artificial device. It is not contrivance. It is natural. In the sense, it is inherent in mans nature. Language is a medium of communication. Man is communicating and gregarious. He is born in the society he can live there. Society, state is natural. The individual and the state are not antagonistic and are mutually complementary. Law is the fulfilment of man's desire. Law is an extraneous restraint. It is an instrument of self realisation. Through the state, laws man attains his highest virtue. The end of the state includes all lesser ends, the family or the village. They are the royal gateway to excellence.

Man can think. Reason is a distinctive quality of the human soul. State is evolutionary from the base family, village constitute state. Family expands into a village, the villages expand into a state. The state continues to grow from family, village etc. He argues men and women come together naturally not deliberately, motivated by the instinct of self-preservation. Sex is the manifestation of this basic instinct. Similarly, it is natural that some people are superior others are inferior. In other words, the family arises out of those two relationships—that between men and women and that between master and slaves. Family forms the village, villages forms the state. The child came to be only through the agency of an actually existing human father. Similarly, man can come only to be through the agency of an actually existing state. State is therefore lies in human nature. The origin of state therefore lies in human nature. The state is a creation of nature. Aristotle is deductive.

Aristotle gives the following arguments to prove that 'The state is a natural institution':

1. Man is a social and political animal—Aristotle believes that man is a political animal, destined by nature for political life. Man is a social animal. He who can live alone is either a beast or a God.

2. Satisfaction of two important instincts—instinct of reproduction and instinct of self preservation—The instinct of reproduction brings the family into existence and the instinct of self-preservation results in the master-slave relationship. The master who is superior in intelligence has the right to employ a slave who is useful to him because he is sturdy in body. The individual depends for the satisfaction of his needs on the family because no individual is self-sufficient. The family is self-sufficient to a degree only. It still needs support from without. Just as the individuals combine to form a family, the families combine to form a village for the better satisfaction of their wants and the villages combine to form a state.[9]

   The state is the logical development of the family. The family is a natural institution. Therefore, the state is a natural institution.

3. The nature of a thing is realised when it reaches the end—Man is a national animal. His true nature is realised only in the state.

4. The state prior to the family and the individual—According to Aristotle, the state is clearly prior to the family and the individual just as a whole is prior to the

part. Aristotle gives the following argument to prove that the whole to prior is the part.

Body is the whole, foot is the part. If the body is destroyed, there is no foot, because it becomes lifeless, has no working power and is foot only in name.

5. The individual has no existence, when separated from the state-just as a part of the body has no existence when separated from the body, similarly the individual when separated from the state cannot exist.

**Nature and End of the State**

Reason expresses the gift of speech. Animals have mere sound which can only convey pleasure or pain. Reason and the power of speech can enable a man to distinguish the right from wrong, just from unjust, good from evil. The state is therefore, natural and is a moral entity. It aims at highest good. He viewed state as an organism. If body is destroyed hand is no longer a hand. A hand so to say, is defined by its function or end or purpose. This function can be performed only if it is joined to a livingbody. Individual is to the state, what a hand is to the body. He cannot fulfilled his good life apart from the state. Make the state healthy, the individual also becomes healthy.

Thus, according to Aristotle, without state its law, its justice, man is the worst of animals. Law is the breath of the state. It exists for the sake of good life. In the sense, happy and honourable life. The state to him is self-sufficing.[10]

**Functions of the State**

Aristotle gives his views about the functions of the state in his book 'The Politics'. According to Aristotle, the state is an association—an association of human beings and the highest form of association.

We can understand Aristotle's philosophy about the functions of the state if we divide the whole of this discussion in the following paragraphs :

1. The state is an association.

2. The state is the supreme associations—highest form of community.
3. The state exists for the supreme good.

**1. The State is an Association**

According to Aristotle, the state is an association. In Greek language, the word used by Aristotle for association is fellowship or partnership. Unlike persons join together and form the state. The state is a plurality. The state according to Aristotle is the result of the social, political and rational nature of man. It is an association of the individuals the families and the villages. The process of formation of the state as an association may be explained by describing the following stages in the process.

***(i) The Family*** : The first association formed by man is the family. The family is the result of the desire to satisfy reproductive instinct. The instinct for self-preservation results in the master slave relationship. In the family, the individual not only gets a chance to satisfy his physical needs but also learns civic virtues. In the family, the individual learns fellowship, political organization and justice which are very essential elements of the state.

***(ii) The Village*** : The family, however, is not adequate for the satisfaction of all the needs of the individual. Just as the individual is not self-sufficient and feels the need of the family for the satisfaction of his needs, similarly, the family is not self-sufficient and there is the need of a higher association. Thus, the process of forming association continues and many families combine to form a village.

***(iii) The State*** : Yet, the process of forming associations does not stop here, because the villages also do not prove adequate for the satisfaction of all the needs. Hence, the process of forming associations continues and many villages join together to form a state.

**2. The State is the Supreme Association**

According to Plato, the state is the supreme association. It is the highest of all the associations. It includes all other associations. The individual is the lowest, step in the ladder which leads to the state. Higher than the individual is the family. Still higher is the village. At the top of all is the state. A simple diagram can explain this idea.

The State
↑
The Village
↑
The Family
↑
The Individual

The state is the largest circle and includes the villages, the families and the individuals.

**The State Aims at the Highest Good**

The state is the supreme association because it aims at the highest good. The highest good is the good life of the citizen. Every other association aims at some particular good which is indeed inferior to the highest good at which the state aims.[11]

**Man's True Nature is Realised Only in the State**

The state is the highest association, in the sense that man's true nature is realised only in the state. In the family, man gets the satisfaction of having children. In the village, his wants are satisfied and he also has the satisfaction of having companions. In the state alone, he gets an opportunity for the right development of his personality. Man's social, political and rational nature is fully realised in the state.

**The State is the Final and Perfect Form of Human Association**

According to Aristotle, the state is the final and perfect form of association. No other association is higher than and superior to the state. The state manifests man's perfect nature. The state is at the top of all other associations like the families etc. Therefore, it aims at the most important good.

**The State is a Whole, the Individuals and Associations are Parts**

According to Aristotle, the state is the whole. The individuals, the family, and the village are the parts. The whole is prior to the parts. The parts are significant because of the idea of the whole. In the order of time the family and the village precede the whole. In order of thought, the state is prior to both the family and the village.

**3. The State Exists for the Supreme Good**

According to Aristotle, the state is a supreme association. It exists not only for life, but for good life. Good life, according to Aristotle means moral life. According to Aristotle, the following alone are not sufficient functions of the state. There are other higher and nobler functions than these.

The state is not merely for war or trade, not a mere insurance against insecurity of life and property.

According to Aristotle, the state does not exist merely for war or trade. Nor is the state an insurance against insecurity of life and property. It does not exist merely for treaties. It does not exist only for security against injustice.

**The Functions of the State is not Mere Protection of Rights**

According to Aristotle the state is supreme association. It exists not only for life, but for good life. Good life, according to Aristotle means moral life.

According to Aristotle, the function of the state is not merely to protect the rights of the individuals against attack by others. The main function of the state is to make its citizens good or to give them education in virtue. To prevent a criminal from committing a crime by fear of punishment does not really sake him a good man. The proper method to improve the people is to educate them in morality. 'Virtue is the case of a true state.' To Aristotle, state perform some positive functions. The state is the school of the citizens. Aristotle believes that the state is an educational institution whose main function is to train the citizens for moral life. The state is all all-in-all for the individuals and promotes their moral well-being. The state which does not promote the moral welfare of the individuals is no state. According to Aristotle, goodness is already there in human nature. It is the duty of the state to develop this goodness through a proper process of education.

**Aristotle's Best State**

Aristotle said, rule of law is a rule of reason. Law is reason. It is neutral, it is just. Custom is a better guide than a law. If ruler is more flexible, it is better than written law. Two good men are always better than one, and therefore, more merrier. If a person sees better with two eyes than the one, hear better with two ears than with one, act better with hands and feet than with one. It is certain that the principle of the many is superior to the principle of the 'one'. Whenever and wherever men are alike or equal, it is neither expedient nor just that one man should be lord of all. If one ruler is thoroughly virtuous, he becomes a God among men and he can rule certainly forever not inturn but always. An ideal state is an aspiration only. We must avoid the extremes, follow the principle of 'golden mean.' That principle led to authority and can led to stability.

In every state Aristotle says there are three classes—the very rich, the very poor and the middle class[12] (the mean). Those who are very rich excel in beauty, strength, birth or wealth, they grow haughty, arrogant, violent and criminal. Those who are very poor, very weak, ugly, victims of inferiority complex, jealous, intriguing, rogues and petty rascals. The first cannot obey the law, the second tend to break them. The government by the rich becomes despotic, government by the poor despicable. In either case, the state will remain divided by conflicts, jealousies, bitterness, and flictions. It will not be one city but two externally at war with each other. The two is divided into rival camps. The best course, therefore, is that the law of the 'Golden Mean' is followed. Government must be run by the middle class citizens who will neither favour the rich nor the poor and who will lean on both. They neither covet nor plot. Their power is transformed into authority. Middle class is the most important source of stability. Neither the rich nor the poor will ever consent to rule intern because they mistrust one another. The middle class is an arbiter. The rule of the middle class is the best admixture of political elements. It is the 'Golden Mean.'

Such a rule ensures liberty as well as equality. Liberty implies that everyone must be able to rule and to be ruled inturn. This is justice. Liberty is based on justice and justice is distributive. If the personal merit and personal contribution of both are equals, they will receive equal amounts. Thus, according to Aristotle, the government by the middle classes is the best form of government. And if it is to be well-ordered its three elements must function is a co-ordinated manner. The relationship of these three elements determines the nature of the government. This elements are :

1. **The deliberative**—In modern parlance legislative which is the supreme element,
2. **The magistracy**—Executive, and the
3. **Judicial**—Whatever the form of government these elements persist.

Aristotle is against the extreme rule of the rich. He is also against the extreme rule of the poor. His opinion is that the rich are very proud and cannot obey. The poor are slavish and cannot command. Aristotle follows the middle path. He recommends the rule of the middle class.

We can draw the following inferences from the above paragraph.

**1. Very Rich People are Very Proud**

Aristotle makes it sufficiently clear in this passage that extremely rich people become extremely proud and arrogant. Their pride is the cause of their unwillingness to obey authority. Hence, there cannot be an ideal government when extremely rich people rule. Oligarchy cannot be an ideal form of government.

**2. Very Poor People are Slavish and Subservient**

Another implication in Aristotle's passage is that extremely poor people so slavish and subservient that they cannot command. There cannot be an ideal government if the extremely poor rule because the poor do not possess the capacity rule. Democracy cannot be an ideal form of government.

**3. A Person Belonging to the Middle Class has the Capacity to Rule**

Aristotle is of opinion that only a person belonging to the middle class, who is neither extremely rich nor extremely poor, but has sufficient property for leading of a life of leisure and virtue knows how to rule and how to obey. A person belonging to the middle class knows how to rule and how to be ruled in turn.

**4. The Rule of the Middle Class is the Best**

Aristotle comes to the conclusion that an ideal state in which the middle class is in a majority. Rule of the middle class is the best. In other words, polity is the best form of government. Polity combines the principles of both oligarchy and democracy. It is free from the vices of oligarchy and democracy. Polity is a balanced and stable state. The dangers of revolutions are farless in a polity than in an oligarchy or democracy.

**5. Mixed Constitution**

According to Aristotle, polity or mixed constitution is the best. It is a compromise between the two extremes—extreme poverty and extreme wealth. It is a compromise between oligarchy and democracy. It combines the principles of both and avoids the vices of both. It brings about a reconciliation between the claims of the rich and the poor to power.

**Material Conditions of the Best State**

We may mention the following conditions, factors and special features of Aristotle's best state.

**1. Population**

A good citizen is identifiable. He said population of the state must be neither too large to kept in order or known to each other nor too small to be inadequate for its civic functioning. Population must be kept under limits. This can be done by fixing the rate of reproduction, by allowing and encouraging infertility among married couples. If no restriction is imposed on the rate of re-production, says Aristotle poverty is inevitable result, and poverty in turn, civic dissension and wrong doing. Regulation of property is meaningless if the number of children exceeds. It is absorbed.

It is necessary that population is held in check. Infact, mortality as a means of population check is not allowed by Aristotle. It is permissible to prevent the growth of deformed children. The size of the family must be fixed beyond it must result in abortion sanctioned by the state. Unlimited population not only brings about economic rain, but it also leads to extreme democracy whose backbone is the mass of people. The population of the state must be sufficient enough both qualitatively and quantitatively.

**2. Territory**

Just the size of the population must be moderate, so the size of the territory. It should just enable the citizen to live a life of leisure, liberty. It should be surveyable and identifiable. According to Aristotle, an ideal state or best state should be so large that the citizens can lead a life of freedom and leisure. The territory of the state should not be so big as big as to encourage luxury. Aristotle recommends the principle of moderation in this respect.

The size of the city-state should be so large as to enable the citizens to earn their livelihood and also to find leisure for reflection and for performance of their civic duties. According to Aristotle, the size of the state should give an opportunity to its citizens to lead a life of temperance.

Aristotle is of opinion that the best state must neither too small nor too large. In case it is too small it will lack of independence. If it is too large, it will lack unity. In determining the size of the territory of the state, Aristotle applies the doctrine of the mean—the middle path. The state according to him, should be neither too small nor too large in area.

**3. Social Structure**

Aristotle's Ideal State or 'Best State' would have a well knit social structure. The integral ports are the citizens. The slavery, artisans and women are the necessary conditions. The ends and objectives of the social structure must be to ensure the services of food, agricultural tools arts crafts, arms, defence, property, land ownership, service of God, public worship, political deliberations and settlement of disputes. The numerous classes of the state therefore, will be the farmers, the artisans, the soldiers, the traders, the priests and the statesmen. Aristotle argues that agriculture and arts cannot be rendered by the citizens. Defence, public worship and political deliberations can be the legitimate sphere of the citizens, provided that defence will be the responsibility of the young citizens, politics would be the preoccupation of the middle aged and public worship of the old and the aged. The remaining service *viz,* property, trade and land ownership should be assigned to the entire body of full citizens. By this ordering of classes, the state will be able to attain the greatest felicity. Land should not be entirely owned in common. Some should be publicly owned and for public worship and the rest should be privately owned. The private owners may have two plots—one near the 'polis' and the other on the frontier.

This arrangement will satisfy the claims of equality and justice. All lands should be cultivated by the slaves or barbarian serfs. Ownership of land should be vested in the soldiers and the statesmen.

**4. Lay-out of the State**

The planning of the city should be determined mainly by considerations of such factors as health, defence, convenience of political activities and a beauty of appearance. As far as health is concerned, it requires a good exposure as well as good water supply Defence city should be planned. The state should be fortified. The walls must always be kept in good order both from the point of view of beauty as well as security. Separate recreation grounds should be maintained for different age groups.

**5. Education**

In the best state, very careful attention ought to be given to education, which is the source of knowledge which can produce goodness and felicity. The education must cover the whole life and all its aspects action and leisure, war and peace. War is a means to peace and action is a means to leisure. The state policy must conform this principle. It should cover different parts of the soul and their different activities. The general aim of the education should not be war oriented. War training is necessary. Leisure would require temperance, courage, endurance and wisdom without which no work can be done an no leisure can be obtained. All this can be achieved by natural endowment *i.e.* physical layout, proper population, territory and social structure. By habit, by education and training these must begin since birth. To have good children, marriages must be carefully planned and regulated to ensure that both men and women do not have divergence of physical power and may procreate soundly. The gap in age should not be very wide and very narrow. It should be a difference of 20 years men at the age of 37 and women at 18. The union of young parents produces females and diminutive figure.[13]

Young mothers die of hard labour pains, young women are also intemperate once they experience sex intercourse. Young men only stunt their growth if they have sex before they fully develop. Children must be given physical exercises, but these should not be arduous or violent. Pregnant mothers must take exercises regularly and should be made to walk daily to the temples for the goodness of child birth. They should be given nourishing diets. The size of the family must be regulated and beyond a fixed number of children. Abortions must be induced. Men should not produce children after the age of 50-55.

Upto the age of 5, children should be given prescribed diet and must be carefully handled and protected from exposure. They should be made to play the games which should be neither laborious nor effeminate. Stories and tales must be carefully selected by the superintendents of education. Children must be encouraged to sob and cry as these give exercises to the lungs. They should be forbidden to abuse or use bad language or even hearing of it and the delinquents must be punished either corporally or through indignities. Children should not be exposed to indecent pictures and plays. The seeing of mimicries and comedies should be forbidden to young persons.[14]

From the age of 5 to 7, children should watch other at work on the lessons which they will afterwards have to learn themselves. From 7 to 14 and from 1 to 21 are the next two phases of education which must be adapted to the constitution, for, a citizen does not belong to himself, he belongs to the state. Education must be regulated by the state. Through laws special emphasis must be given to reading and writing, drawing, gymnastic and music. The first two are useful in practical life. Gymnastic's promote's courage and music enables one to enjoy leisure which is higher than occupation and which is the end to which occupation is directed. Reading and writing make it possible to acquire the branches of knowledge. Drawing enables us to judge more correctly. The works of different artists and saves us from making mistakes in private purchases. Aristotle advises that excessive early physical training which stunts the proper development of the body and mind must be avoided. Till the age of puberty, exercises should be light and there should be no rigorous dieting. Then for three years the child should study reading, writing, music, drawing, followed for a period of hard work or exercise and strict diet.[15]

Aristotle has attached very great importance to music which he considers to be the pivot of education. It is only a source of amusement and relaxation. It serves as a means of moral training and cultivation of mind and growth of moral wisdom. Music whether vocal or instrumental is not only one of the greatest of pleasures and relaxations, but it has also a higher value. Music says Aristotle is a source of delight. Delight is caused by goodness. Music is therefore, akin to goodness. Music rouses right emotions about good and bad actions, good and bad characters. Musical tunes and melodies produce image of states of character, anger, calm, fortitude, temperance and the sould can really undergo a change by right music. Thus, Aristotle argues that music possesses the power of producing an effect on the character of the soul and it must be made a subject of study for the young. The modes and rhythms of music have an affinity with the soul. The young must taught to play music otherwise, they will not be able to judge a performance. But they should not be professionals. Their interest should only be to appreciate good melodies and rhythms and they need not involve themselves in different compositions or any occupations which he will make them vulgar. They should also avoid playing on flutes or harps which do not express a state of character, but only a mood of religious excitement and which prevent the player from using his voice.

And finally importance must be attached to these melodies, which are expressive of character, if education is the objective of music. But the music has two other objectives—the release of emotion, recreation and relaxation. There are certain melodies which produce inspiration and which stimulate action.

Thus, Aristotle concludes, that education must be controlled by the state. It should be adapted to the form of government. The citizen, so to say, must be moulded to the form of government under which he lives. Education is great mover and pusher of forces. Education also inculcates obedience to law for he who cannot obey, cannot command. Only a state controlled education can lead to social and political unity.

**6. Good Climate Conditions**

According to Aristotle, another very important condition for the best state is that the climate of the state should be congenial for the physical and mental health of the people. The climate of the state should be neither too hot nor too cold. A temperate climate is most suitable for the physical, mental, moral and material development of the people.

### 7. Character of the People

According to Aristotle, an ideal state is that in which the citizens possess a very high character. Pursuit of virtue is an essential condition for the best life. Pursuit of virtue is better, higher and nobles than power of wealth. The citizens should lead a happy and balanced life. They should pursue external goods of the body and goods of the soul in a balanced manner. They should not run too much after the external goods and the goods of the body. They should pursue the true end of human life—the goods of the soul. Aristotle believes that only the Greeks are capable of exhibiting the qualities of exalted character, and of pursuing a life of virtue.

### 8. Policy of Peace

According to Aristotle, an ideal state is one which follows the policy of peace and avoids war. An ideal state is not aggressive in its policy. It has not imperialistic designs. It does not attack other countries. It's aim is not to capture the territories of other states, but to promote the virtuous, happy and good life of the people.[16]

### 9. Classes in the Best State-Performance of Different Services in the Best State

According to Aristotle the state consists of the following classes or elements. These classes make the state self-sufficing. The ideal state is divided into various classes : 1. Agriculturists, 2. Artisans, 3. Warriors, Well-to-do people having leisure, 5. Priests and 6. Administrations.

### Services and Functions Performed on the Basis of Age

In the best state, the functions are performed by the citizens on the basis of their age. Aristotle assigns the following duties to different age groups.

1. Young people must render military service. Defence of the country is their duty. The warriors must belong to the younger generation.

2. Persons belonging to middle age must perform the duties of administration. Administrators must be middle-aged persons.
3. Religious duties must be performed by old people.

The priests must be old people

This arrangement, according to age-groups gives a chance to all the citizens to make their contribution to different functions at the proper time of their age depending upon their training, experience and temperament.

**10. Small City-State**

According to Aristotle, the ideal state is a small city-state. The individual can develop their best selves only in a city-state. Moral improvement is possible only in a city-state. A big state cannot give best opportunities to the citizens for their moral development. The community must be a city and not a people.[17]

## ARISTOTLE'S THEORY OF CITIZENSHIP

**Introduction**

In ancient Greek city-states the citizens were the privileged people. They could participate in the affairs of the state, whereas the slave and the aliens could not. The Greeks did not think of citizenship in terms of rights. They thought that citizenship afforded them an opportunity to serve the state. For the Greeks, the state was "a partnership in a life of virtue" According to him, a citizen is one who shares in the administration of justice and in the offices. Aristotle proceeds population in a state can be divided into two parts. First those who constitute its essence and core are its integral parts. They are the citizens. Secondly, those who are not its core, they provide material basis to the state. But they are not directly participate in political activity. They are not called the citizens. Aristotle is an objective philosopher and inductive approach to politics. Citizen is a man who shares in the administration of justice and in the holding of office *i.e.* One who can hold the office of the judge, and membership of the assembly. The number of such persons can be neither too small nor too big.[18]

Those who enjoys the right in deliberative and judicial office for a period, attains thereby the status of a citizen of his state. Aristotle's citizen will be in tune with the voice of human reason, will be capable of facing facts, opinions, traditions. Those who are incapable of thinking or reasoning, such persons are not citizens. Aristotle said state is a compound. Man's mind is heterogeneous and family is composite. The state also is made up of many parts which are unequal. Aristotle calls the state 'a compound' in the sense of whole not in the sense of aggregate. A aggregate is merely a crowd, a heap, a mechanical assemblage. A whole is organic, the 'polis' is a whole not an aggregate, and whole has a core and circumference. The core is active, it is sovereign element. The circumference is the passive subject—the ruled. A 'polis' is composed of unlike elements. It is composed of different elements *i.e.* husband and wife, master and slave, but also other's in addition *i.e.* ruler and ruled, parent and child, soldier and civilian. A state is a compound made up of citizens. The citizens thus, provides the human basis to state.[19]

But everyone living with the polis is not a citizen. Citizenship is not based on residence in a given place, because residents, aliens, slaves lives in a common place. But that does not make them citizens at all. The citizen are those who live a higher life. Those who have acquired constitutional eights, they are the citizens. The citizens must have excellence. But this excellence is relative to the constitution. If there are different kinds of constitution, excellence of the citizen must also differ. Citizens have to perform different tasks under a common leader. They must have the capacity of leading as well as that of being led, of ruling as well as that of being ruled. But the good citizen must possess the knowledge and the capacity requisite for ruling as well as for being ruled.

Aristotle's theory of citizenship is related to his view of good life, his theory of souls and his theory of causes. He also prescribes objective tests for citizenship—both negative and positive. His theory of citizenship is restrictive and is a mirror of the conditions prevailing in ancient Greece.

## QUALIFICATIONS FOR A CITIZEN

According to Aristotle a citizen must possess the following qualifications :

### 1. Capacity to Rule and to be Ruled

According to Aristotle, a citizen must have the capacity to rule and willingness to be ruled. In order to be a citizen, it is essential that the person must be a good ruler and must be an obedient subject. It is the duty of the law-maker to obey the law. The citizen must know how to command and also must know how to obey. The possession of only one of these two qualities does not make a man a citizen. One who knows how to command and has not learn how to obey cannot be a good citizen. One who only knows how to obey and does not knowhow to rule is also not a good citizen. Command and obedience go together. Both are important qualities or virtues of a citizen. Aristotle says "It has been well said, he who has never learnt to obey cannot be a good commander". The two are not the same, but the good citizen ought to be capable of both.

### 2. The Citizen should have Leisure

Aristotle says that in order to be a citizen a man should have some leisure. The importance of leisure to develop the personality of the individual has been recognized by all thinkers. Without leisure, a man cannot be his best self. Without leisure we cannot discover the land of our mind. Life of toil, without leisure is a poor life. To us, leisure means the time when we are free from the routine work. The students, the teachers, the office clerks, the officers, and the labourers all have their leisure and ought to have it. Leisure is used in our days to have recreation in order to be fresh for the next day's work.[20]

Aristotle understood leisure in a different sense. For him, leisure did not mean relaxation. It was a form of activity. According to Aristotle, there were two types of activities. One, work which is not an end in itself, but which is a means to an end. This work is done because it is useful and necessary. To illustrate work of this type, Aristotle gives the examples of ploughing, making garments etc. Second, some activities are ends in themselves. Pursuing knowledge, painting, writing poems, music etc. are such activities. Pursuit of higher values of truth, beauty and goodness is an activity which is an end in itself. Such an activity is leisure for Aristotle.

**Leisure Essential to Enable a Man to Rule Well**

Aristotle suggests that magistrates should be chosen not only on the basis of their merit, but also on the basis of wealth in their possession. A poor man cannot rule well because he has no leisure.[21]

**3. The Citizen should have Property**

Aristotle regards leisure as very essential for citizenship. Leisure is possible only when a man has property. Therefore, property is very essential for citizenship.

## PERSONS EXCLUDED FROM CITIZENSHIP

Aristotle is of opinion that the following persons are not the citizens. Aristotle excludes these persons from citizenship and assigns reasons for excluding them.

**1. Women**

Aristotle excludes women from citizenship. He regards them inferior to men. According to him, women's sphere is the home and silence her chief virtue. Aristotle says, the male is by nature superior and the female inferior and the one rules and the other is ruled. According to Aristotle, the duties of men and women are different. He says, the part of men and women in the management of the household is different. The duty of the one is to acquire, of the other is to preserve.

Women is regarded by Aristotle as a means not as an end. It is natural women is inferior to men. The one rules and the other is ruled. Women must stay at home, keep the house and tend their husbands and children. They are not fitted by nature for public life. A man is a brave and the women is a chatter box. The male is active, formative principle, female is passive clay waiting to be formed. Women is weak of will and incapable of independence of character or position, while men will rule her in there external relations. She may be supreme in domestic sphere.

Due to women's inferiority that Aristotle suggests men should not marry till the age of 37 and then with a girl of 20 years. Such a marriage would give an indispensable advantage to men. If the men is still able to beget children while the women is unable to bear them says Aristotle or vice versa quarrels and differences will arise. The union of male and female when too young is bad for the creation of children. In all animals the offspring's of the young are small and ill-developed generally female. Aristotle disregarded the principle of equality. He proceeds to argue that equals should be treated equally and unequal unequally. In this content no justice is involved. Injustice, he says, would arise as much from treating unequal equals as from treating equals unequally. The women is the modest of silence should nurse the children, receive and comfort their husbands. Women are weak. Men acquires, women keeps and stores. Women is fit to be ruled and she help a men to rule. But she herself is incapable of participating in political life.

**2. The Slaves**

The slaves are not the citizens. A slave is a part of the property of the householder. He is an animate instrument of action. A slave occupies a position between the men and the beast. He has no reason of his own. He cannot direct himself. He is inferior in intelligence. He is physically strong and fit and nature has made him fit for manual work only. He has no leisure. He cannot participate in the affairs of the state. From the hour of his birth he is born a slave to be ruled by master who is superior to him in intelligence.

Who is a slave? Who can own him? Aristotle says he who is by nature not his own. Slave is inferior to the master. Slavery is both right and expedient. Slaves should not be Greeks, but an inferior race. Inferior are ruled by the superiors. Slavery is justified both for a slave as well as the master. The slave are fit for the physical activity. In a healthy individual soul rules the body and the intellect rules appetites. If the order is reversed health would be ruined. Similarly men rules the animals. In both cases the body and the animal have physical functions and can do noting better. The master had almost absolute control over him life and limb. The soul Aristotle says rules the body with a despotic rule. The relation is natural.

**3. The Labourers and the Mechanics**

According to Aristotle, the labourers and mechanics are not the citizens. They are so busy in producing necessary things for subsistence that they have not leisure. Hence, they are not entitled to participation in the matters of the state. Manual labourers and mechanics do not act with mind, only with body. They live by their hands, and such a life is ignoble, inimical to virtue. They have not leisure and cannot contemplate. They are therefore, by nature uncivil and cannot be admitted to the core of polity.

**4. Persons who Acquire Wealth by Unnatural Methods**

The unnatural method is for the sake of accumulation. Wealth earned from the trade is hateful, because it is unnatural. But the most hateful method of earning money is usury because it is unnatural breeding of money out of money. According to Aristotle, trade and barter carried on with the sole aim of amassing money and lending money on interest are unnatural methods of acquiring wealth. Aristotle thinks that all such persons as are engaged in acquiring wealth by unnatural methods are not entitled to citizenship. Money is the sole aim of their life. They are the lovers of money and not of men. They have no leisure. They have no virtue. Hence, they cannot participate in state matters. They are not the citizens.

**5. Old Persons**

According to Aristotle, old people are not entitled to citizenship because they are too feeble in body and mind to participate in state matters. Those who are old enough to have been excused from the civic duties. They have no claim to citizenship.

**6. Children**

Children are not entitled to become citizens. Children are not fully developed mentally and physically to participate in state affairs. Children are not citizens. They may be citizens in the making. They are too young to be entered on the rolls of citizens.

**7. Aliens or Foreigners**

Aliens are not citizens, because they are not loyal and patriot to the state. They are the lovers of their own country. That is why they are not citizens says Aristotle.

## CRITICISMS OF ARISTOTLE'S THEORY OF CITIZENSHIP

Aristotle is very famous in the history of political thought for his views about the nature of the state, his view about property and slavery. Similarly, his views about citizenship are also well known. He has made a great contribution to political thought.

But in spite of greatness in his political thought, we find several defects in his theory of citizenship. Some of the defects in his theory of citizenship are given below :

**1. Aristotle's Concept of Citizenship is Very Narrow and Limited**

Aristotle's concept of citizenship is narrow and limited. He includes only a part of the population in the list of citizens and excludes quite a major portion from this list. He excludes all mechanics, labourers and manual workers from citizenship. There can be no justification of denying to this group of people who produce necessary things. In modern times, the labourers and the mechanics etc. are citizens like other people. Aristotle excludes women from the class of citizens. This is gross injustice. Aristotle is not right in believing that women are inferior to men. He is not correct in believing that women's sphere is the home.

Aristotle's view about women is too conservative to be applicable in modern times. Women are not kept within the four walls of the home. They have been emancipated and are playing a leading role in all walks of life all over the world. Women today have the right to vote and are making a remarkable contribution to the social and political life of their countries. We can say that Aristotle's theory of citizenship is too conservative and too aristocratic to have any relevance in modern times.

**2. Aristotle Attaches too much Importance to Property**

Aristotle thinks that only men having property can be citizens. He argues that propertyless people cannot be the citizens because they have no interest and no experience in the management of the state affairs. This is fallacious reasoning. To give right of citizenship to property holders is to create a class government. Such a government will always favour the property holders and will ignore the interests of the propertyless people.

This is a gross injustice and is against the modern democratic and socialistic ideas of equality. To make property an essential condition for citizenship is to create a class of aristocrats to rule over the propertyless people. This is injustice to a very important part of the population of the state.

**3. Aristotle's Theory of Citizenship is inconsistent with his wwn theory of the State as an Organic Unity**

In his theory of citizenship, Aristotle contradicts his own theory of the state as an organic unity. On the one hand, Aristotle says that the state is an organic unity. On the other hand, he creates two divisions in the state-citizens and non-citizens. He excludes a substantial portion of the population of the state from citizenship. The labourers, the mechanics, women and traders etc. are not the citizens. Aristotle himself admits that the working classes are essential to the states existence but at the same time says that this does not constitute them citizens. In this way, he contradicts his own views. According to Aristotle, the individuals are parts of the state which is an organic whole. He is unkind and unjust to a vast population of the state the workers, the mechanics and the manual workers and deprives them of the right of citizenship.

### 4. Aristotle's View that the Citizen must Function as a Juror or a Legislator does not have Universal Application

Aristotle defines citizenship in terms of functions performed by the individual. He is of opinion that the citizen must be Juror or a legislator. These functions have a restricted application. They are not universal application. For example, the Jury system does not exist in all the states. Infact, Aristotle's theory is applicable only to the city-states of Athens. It does not have a universal application.

### 5. Aristotle's Theory of Citizenship is not Applicable to the Modern State

Aristotle's theory of citizenship is not applicable to the modern state. The modern state has a large population. Aristotle's definition of citizenship cannot cover the circle of citizens in the modern state. The number of the jurors and the legislators in the modern state is only a very small part of the total population of the state. If we accept Aristotle's theory of citizenship today, millions of people will be excluded from citizenship.

### 6. Aristotle's Theory of Citizenship not Applicable to Representative or Indirect Democracy

We are living in an age of indirect or representative democracy in which only a few hundred representatives of millions of people are the legislators. Athenian democracy in Aristotle's times was direct democracy in which all the citizens participated in the affairs of the government. The number of the citizens in Aristotle's days was equal to the number of the legislators and the jurors. In our times the number of citizens is much larger than the number of the legislators and the jurors. The modern states have granted the right of citizenship to all adult men and women irrespective of their occupations and property qualifications.

### 7. Aristotle is Unjust to the Labourers, Manual Workers and Mechanics etc.

Aristotle has a very poor opinion about the labourers,

mechanics and the manual workers and excludes them from the class of citizens. The labourers the mechanics and manual workers produce necessities of life. There is no justification for looking down upon the labourers, the mechanics and the manual workers etc. To deprive such a useful section of the population of the city-state of the right of citizenship is injustice. It is not correct to think that the labourers, mechanics and manual workers have no virtue and are incapable of becoming citizens.

## ARISTOTLE'S CONCEPT OF REVOLUTION

### Introduction

Men when under the wings of reason, is the best of creations, but when cut off from it, he is the worst of all. Injustice is most dangerous when armed. Since birth, men is equipped with the weapons of intelligence. It is only in the state that man can attain virtue. Men's reason is communicable through speech which is the golden thread weaving society. Society is the mother of intelligence, which in its turn gives birth to order. It is only in the society, men can climb the highest of glory and culture and can achieve the best of which he is capable. One who lives outside society is either a beast or a God. Stability is wished for, revolution is order.

In book V of the politics, Aristotle discusses one of the most important problems which the rulers have to often face. This is the problem of revolutions and how to prevent them. In discussing this problem, Aristotle shows a vast knowledge of the subject. He studied the constitutions of 158 states in details. Aristotle had observed changes in the constitutions of different city-states. This observation went a long way to help him to discuss the problem of the causes of revolutions and the methods of checking them. Aristotle studied the whole of this problem scientifically, systematically and empirically. He applied inductive reasoning in studying this problem. In other words, he first observed the happenings and changes in different city-states and tried to find out the causes and suggest remedies of revolutions. He drew conclusions from the observation of facts.[22]

Aristotle gave the meaning of revolution. He discussed the general causes of revolution and also the particular causes. Aristotle's treatment of the subject is objective and scientific. In that part of politics in which Aristotle discussed the problems of revolutions, we notice a tendency on his part to separate ethics from politics.

**Meaning of Revolution**

For Aristotle revolution has two meanings. These two meanings of revolution as understood by Aristotle are given below :

**1. Change in the Constitution**

Aristotle says that in case, there is a big or even a small change in the constitution, a revolution has occurred. For example, a change from monarchy to aristocracy means a revolution for Aristotle. When democracy becomes less democratic, there is a revolution according to him. Similarly, when oligarchy becomes less oligarchic, a revolution has taken place, according to Aristotle. Thus according to him, the democrats comes in power after overthrowing the oligarchs. The oligarchs become the rulers after over throwing the democrats. Thus, we find that the first meaning of revolution according to Aristotle, is the minor or major change in the constitution.[23]

**2. Change in the Rulers**

Even when there is no change in the constitution, but, there is a change only in the rulers, the change means revolution, according to Aristotle. In other words, when the power of governing the country passes from the hands of one person to another person, there is a revolution. If one monarch is removed from power and another takes his place, there is a revolution. If one tyrant has to surrender power to another tyrant, there is revolution.

Revolution had a broader meaning for Aristotle. It means more than a political change. Aristotle gave a broader meaning to revolution than what we understand by revolution in modern times. A change in the constitution was not merely a political change. Revolution for Aristotle was not merely a political change, it meant social and moral changes also. A change in the constitution had great moral and social significance. It meant new social and moral ways of life.[24]

## CAUSES OF REVOLUTION

### General Causes

When political order faits to the distribution of property, tensions arise which eventually lead to revolution. Inequality is the real cause. Superiority and inferiority complex leads to revolution. Inferiors revolt in order that they may be equal and equals that they may be superior. Such is the state of mind which creates revolutions.

Aristotle says there are broadly two factors which lead to revolutions.

### I. Psychological Factors

**1. Profit.** It means that the officers of the state try to make illicit gains at the expense of the individual or the public. It creates a loss and a mood of discontent on the part of the public.

**2. Honour.** It means or it implies that men are dishonoured rightly or wrongly, but see others obtaining honours rightly or wrongly rise in rebellion and like minded people. Join and stress the government to redress such grievances. Unmerited honour is a baneful to stability. It creates a feeling of restlessness.

**3. Insolence.** Insolence of office produces a climate of revolution and if the officers of state become haughty, arrogant and drunk with power instead of listening to the genuine complaints of the people, they will behave with them rudely. A charm would be created between the state and the people. The officers going in one direction and the people in another. Such officers become disloyal to the government and the constitution from which they derive their power and authority. The people therefore, begin murmuring and the murmurs in the huts, cottages, streets and market places rise in a mounting which leads to popular evolution.

**4. Fear.** It is imaginary. It is the worst enemy of men and human institutions. It disturbs the tranquility of mind more than any other emotion. It may be the fear of punishment for a wrong actually committed. It may be the fear of the expected wrong to be inflicted on the person who is afraid of. It leads to revolution.[25]

**5. Superiority complex.** It is imical to cordial social and political relationship. If there are persons for any one or other reasons develops a complex that they are superior to the rest who are inferior to them. It will release a chain of reaction which will ruin the peace of the whole society. Such persons try to concentrate all power in themselves and do not hesitate in misusing it. Whatever they do, they justify whatever cruelties or ill-treatment they inflict on others. They regard both as fair to themselves honourable and all the rest as dishonourable. This is a state of affairs which is conducive to monarchy or oligarchy.

**6. Contempt.** It is a close ally of revolution-contempt for rulers, contempt for laws, contempt for social and political institutions, contempt for social and economic order. The contempt may be produce gross inequalities, the outcome of injustices, the result of arrogance, the offshoot of wealth or economic order, the reaction of privileges given to some or denied to others.

**7. Disappropriate increase in some part of the state.** There would arises a gulf, imbalances between the constitution and the society. After all, constitution is a mirror of social reality. It reflects the balance of social and economic forces. If this balance is disturbed or gets altered, the constitution is shaken to its foundations and will either get modified or perish. If for example, the number of the poor people increases the fabric of the polity may be destroyed. Similarly the rich become more numerous a polity may undergo an upheaval after which it may turn into an oligarchy. Such an increase of a class in society is like the disease, which makes men a animal. Aristotle compared state to body, the body is compared of parts and it must grow proportionately, if symmetry is to be maintained. It will lead to disproportionate increase means of change of equality as well as quantity.

**II. Political Factors**

The seven political factors are :

**1. Election intrigues.** It can destroy the faith of the people in the constitutional process. If they succeed they pervert constitution completely, if they fail, a great damage is done in so far as they shake peoples confidence. They may frustrate the public opinion and may really cause the worst appear the best or *vice-versa*. They destroy the virtue and good life. They generates the germs of corruption, bribary, nepotism and other malpractices.

**2. Carelessness, or willful negligence.** It may also ruin the very foundations of the state. It produces revolutionary situations. If the rulers are careless in the election of officers and magistrates are undesirable, anti-social corrupt, subversive and incompetent persons are allowed to creep in positions of eminence and responsibility. They may subvert the entire constitution. Again, negligence of what may appear to be trifling matter may prove to be more fatal.

**3. Neglect about small matters of trifling changes.** Statesmanship require's that even small matters should not be neglected. If decisions are made in hurry or hasty without considering all its implications. These may create explosive situations. Appearances can be deceptive and a statesmen should be wary and careful.

**4. Dissimilarity of elements in the composition of the state.** It also leads to revolution. When a large segments of population are allowed to immigrate in a body politic, you are asking for an explosive situation, for their modes of living, manners, customs, likes and dislikes. Even dialectics and religion, their thought and attitude may be different and assimilation may be either impossible or painfully slow.

**5. Growth in reputation and power of some office.** Some times feuds and bitter conflicts among leaders and notable may produce a chain reaction in the whole state which may stand divided in two or more camps each supporting its own favourite leader. Discards among the notables he says involve the whole state in their consequences. If one section of the society or one officer or a set of officers is allowed to grow in influence or prestige or reputation so that the person or persons concerned overshadow the rest, a revolution may occur.

**6. An even balance of parties leading to deadlock.** Again in societies where antagonistic sections such as the rich and the poor are evenly balanced and there is no sizeable middle class to till the balance, there revolutionary fires can be kindled. Finally, political revolutions are sometimes achieved by force and sometimes by fraud.

**7. Foreign Influence.** Aristotle also says that all constitutions may be undermined and affected by the influence of powerful neighbouring states. This happens when they are confronted by the constitution, of an opposite type, which is either their close neighbour or powerful even if they distant. The Athenians, for example, everywhere put down oligarchies, the Spartans, in turn suppressed democracies.

### Revolutions are Harmful

Revolutions in any case are harmful and must be avoided. They are harmful in the long run. They may achieve some immediate good, but at the cost of many evils. The direct results of revolution may be tangible and wholesome, but the indirect ones are incalculable and often disastrous. A keen student of political science says, Aristotle not allow himself to be easily deceived by quick hopes, he should take into account all the points before he pronounces judgement.

Aristotle therefore, argues that revolutions must be avoid. But how?

### Method to Prevent Revolutions

The rulers should know that they can fool some people for all the time, all the people for sometime, but not all the people all the time. Again the rulers should keep a kindly eye on everyone under their care. They should not discriminate between the officers and the common people, between the governing classes and the unenfranchised. A democratic spirit of equality must promote the whole body politic.

Every citizen must be given a chance to have a share in the government sometimes or the other and this is possible only if the tenure of office is limited and a short of 6 months. This will prevent oligarchies and aristocracies from falling into the hands of families. They should not give false alarms so that people are always on their guard. Statesmen should keep a constant vigil and not allow quarrels and seditions among the rulers. The rulers should also watch the movement of assessments connected with a requirement of property qualification. No person should be suddenly raised to the heavens and equally suddenly razed to the ground. To give moderate honours for a long-time would be much better than to give spectacular honour for a short time.

Those who have, unfortunately been allowed to accumulate too much power derived either from friends or money should be ostracized and banished. The Magistrate should keep a eye on the movements and activities of the people. A balance between social and economic forces must be maintained. No particular section of society should be allowed to overshadow the rest. To achieve this offices must be given to opposite elements, the rich and the poor which will check and balance each other. The rich and the poor can be combined in one body and the middle class kept in another. This arrangement would eliminate the evil effects of inequality. Democracy and aristocracy would be combined to produce a stable polity. Those officers who do well should be awarded honour's. An aristocratic ruler particularly should appear to be earnest in the worship of the Gods. Rulers should be loyal to the constitution. They should be competent, able, and worthy and the capacity for the duties of high offices. They should have goodness and justice in the particular form. If the persons of all these qualifications are not available, a combination of any two would do for most of the offices. The education is an instrument for curbing the revolutionary instinct and for preserving the social order. There is no profit or gain. The majority of the people will then be in favour of the constitution and against revolution.[27]

## Aristotle's Ideas on Slavery

Aristotle is well known in the history of political thought for his views on slavery. He is in favour of the institution of slavery and gives many arguments to justify it. He does not accept the doctrine of the sophists that slavery is a conventional and artificial institution. He thinks that slavery is a natural institution. He believes that it is a natural distinction. The masters are made by nature superior in intelligence to rule over the slaves who are made by nature inferior in intelligence. According to Aristotle, the slave is a part of the property of the household. He is an animate part, whereas other things and instruments are inanimate parts. The slave is a living instrument, an instrument of action.[28]

## DEFINITION AND DESCRIPTION OF A SLAVE

### 1. Slaves are Inferior, Master are Superior in Intelligence

According to Aristotle, the slave is a tool with life in it and the tool is a lifeless slave. A slave according to Aristotle is one who is inferior in intelligence, but physically strong. He is useful for the master and for himself. The relation between the masters and the slaves is determined by nature. The masters are superior to command and the slaves are the inferior to obey.

### 2. Slaves are Made by Nature

Aristotle thinks that slaves are made by nature, not by any process of law-making by men, or by any convention of men. Nature has intended some men to rule, others to obey. Some are born masters, others are born slaves.

### 3. Slaves must be Non-Greeks

Aristotle pointed out that the Greeks are intellectually superior to other races, therefore, they should hold intellectually inferior people as slaves. In other words, the Greeks must be the masters and the slaves must belong to other races who are less intelligent than the Greeks. When the Greeks defeat the less intelligent races in war, they can capture slaves.

### 4. A Slave is a Living Possession and is Necessary for the Household

Aristotle says in the politics "A complete household consists of slaves and freemen." The first and the fewest possible parts of a family are master and slave, husband and wife, father and children. A slave is a living possession. The master is only the master of the slave, but the slave is not only the slave of the master, but wholly belongs to him. Some should rule and others be ruled is a thing not only necessary, but expedient.

### 5. A Slave Occupies Middle Position Between Men and Animal

According to Aristotle, a slave occupies a middle position between men and animal. He is more than an animal and less than a men. The difference between the slave and the animal is that an animal has no rationality at all. The slave has sufficient reason to comprehend over other men's reason. The slave is less than a man because he cannot reason independently. He is devoid of the capacity of forethought. He is without the capacity of self-direction. He needs direction from superiors.[29]

### 6. A Slave is a Domestic Animal

Aristotle thinks that men is a rational, social and political animal. It is not possible for men to live alone. The men who can live alone is either a beast or a God. According to Aristotle, the slave is a domestic animal. He is at the master's back and call as other animals are. He has to obey his master. He is totally subordinate to him.

### 7. The Slave is Strong in Body the Master is Strong in Intelligence

Aristotle says that the slave is strong physically and is useful for hard labour which requires physical strength. The master is strong in intelligence. Though he cannot do that hard physical labour which the slave can do, yet his superior intelligence makes him useful for political life "in the arts both of war and peace".

**8. The Slave can also have Virtues**

Aristotle asks the question whether a slave can have the virtues of temperance, courage and justice etc. or whether he has only physical qualities to serve his master. The great philosopher is of opinion that the slaves can also be rational human beings, therefore, it is absurd to think that they do not possess virtues. The virtue of a slave is relative to a master. The virtue of a slave is that he should not fail in his duty to his master. He should not show cowardice while performing his duties. His behaviour should not indicate that he lacks self control.

## JUSTIFICATION OF SLAVERY

**Introduction**

In order to understand Aristotle's justification of slavery, it is important to know that slavery was very important institution in ancient Greece. Barker quoting the statistics says that there were thousands of slaves in Athens. Many worked in sliver mines, many were employed by the artisans, and others worked as domestic servants. Most of the Greek citizens possessed slaves. Their importance in the social and economic life of the Athenians was so great that abolition of slavery would have shattered the stability of the Athenian state. The possession of a slave added to the social prestige of the possessor.

Aristotle gives the following arguments in defence of slavery :

**1. A Slave gives Leisure to the Master and Enables him to develop the Moral and Intellectual Excellence of which he is Capable**

Aristotle argues that the possession of slaves enables a men to develop the moral and intellectual excellence because the slave is an instrument of action in the management of the household and, therefore, is the cause of leisure for the master who can devote this leisure to the development of higher moral and intellectual qualities of which he is capable. The master can devote his time and energy to the performance of his energies as a citizen because of the leisure which he has on account of the possession of the slave. The master is free to participate in the state affairs. According to Aristotle, property and leisure are essential conditions of citizenship. A slave is a part of property and a slave gives sufficient leisure to the master. It is clear that Aristotle thinks that in order to be a great citizen, a man must have a slave.

**2. Slavery is in the Interest of the Slave Himself**

Another argument which Aristotle advances to justify slavery is that it is good and useful not only for the master but also for the slave himself. Slavery is in the interest of the slave himself because he gets best and suitable conditions for his life. The excellence of the master is 'derived' by the slave. Since the slave is mentally and intellectually inferior to the master, since the slaves lacks intelligence and can perform only mechanical functions, it is in fitness of things that such men are slaves. They must be subject to direction by a master having moral and intellectual excellence. The slaves benefit from the excellence of the master. A slave does not have the virtue of temperance. In other words, he does not control his appetite by reason.

**3. Slavery Justified by Aristotle on Account of Existing Conditions in Greece**

Slavery was a very important institute on in Greece during the times of Aristotle. In every state of Greece, there were slaves. Even in other parts of the world slavery existed. In Athens alone, there were thousands of slaves. Almost each citizen had a slave. Many of them were workers in silver mines. Many were employed by the artisans and many were domestic servants. The slave had become a significant part of the economic and social life of Athens and other Greek city-states. Aristotle was well aware that good life for the Greek citizens was not possible without the slaves. He knew that so great was the importance of the slaves in the social and economic life of the Greeks and abolition of slavery would have shattered the stability of the Greek city states.[30]

### 4. Men are by Nature Unequal

Aristotle is a critic of the theory of the sophists that slavery is against nature. The sophists believed that all men are born equal and free. Slavery is man-made, artificial and conditional according to them.

According to Aristotle, men are born unequal. The capacity for virtue in men is not equal. It is unequal from the time of their birth. Different persons have been endowed with different qualities. There are physical and mental differences among people. Equality, according to Aristotle, is against the principles of nature. Inequality is in accordance with nature. Some are more intelligent than others. Some are physically stronger. Therefore, some are masters and others are slaves. Intelligence entitles men to be masters physical strength makes them fit for slavery.

### 5. The Superiors Rule Over the Inferiors

According to Aristotle, the whole is made of several parts. To attain the end or purpose of the whole, the superior in nature must rule over the inferior. The inferiors are subordinate. The superiors are the commanders and the rulers. Aristotle points out that the soul rules over the body. Reason rules over appetite. Men rule over tame animals. The male is by nature superior, and the female inferior, and the one rules and the other is ruled. This principle of necessity extends to all mankind. Those who are superior in intelligence are masters. Those who are inferior are slaves. Superior intelligence is the quality of the masters. Physical strength is the quality of the slave. The physically strong, but mentally inferior are commanded and ruled by men whom nature has endowed with a superior intelligence. The slave has no reason of his own, but can comprehend other man's reason. He has to be commanded and directed because he cannot command and direct himself.

**6. Physical Strength makes the Slave Fit for Manual Labour**

Though the slave is intellectually inferior, yet he has a strong point. This strong point is his physical strength. The slaves physical strength enables him to do manual work. "Nature has made the slave strong for servile labour".

**7. The Slave is an Essential Part of the Household or the Family**

The family is a natural institution, therefore, slavery is also a natural institution. According to Aristotle, the family is a natural institution. It is the result of the association of the male and the female for the propagation of the race and the association of the master and the slave for production of subsistence. In a family, there is three-fold relationship—husband and wife relationship, father and child relationship, and the master-slave relationship. Since the family is a natural institution and the slave is a very important part of the family. Aristotle also draws the inference that slavery also is a natural institution.

**8. Aristotle Justified Slavery Because He Thought that the Greeks were Superior to other Races**

Aristotle said in defence of slavery that the Greeks were superior to other races from the cultural, moral and intellectual points of view. He thought that the non-Greeks who were inferior must be made slaves. The Greeks who were superior were justified in making non-Greeks the slaves. He had a very poor opinion about the non-Greeks. The non-Greeks in his opinion were 'barbarians'. The Greeks who were superior were justified in making non-Greeks their slaves. The association of the superiors (The Greeks) as the masters and the inferiors (non-Greeks) as the slaves would be for the good of both.

**9. Slavery, A Social Necessity**

Aristotle thinks that slavery is very useful and helpful for the attainment of perfection in social life. The slave and the master are not opposed to each other. The slave is useful for the master because he provides him leisure and enables him to attain perfection in society from moral and social points of view by enabling him to participate in all state matters. The slave also gains by associating with his master who is superior to him and who provides better conditions of life for him. Thus, both the master and the slave are gainers and the result is social perfection. Therefore, slavery is a social necessity.

**Slavery is justified only Under Certain Conditions**

Aristotle suggests that slavery is justified only when certain conditions are observed. He supports the institution of slavery, but imposes the following conditions for the possession of the slaves.

**1. Only Persons with Low and Inferior Intelligence should be made Slaves**

Aristotle suggests that only persons who are low and inferior in intelligence should be made slaves. He is not in favour of making all prisoners of war, the slaves. He does not like the idea of wholesale enslavement of prisoners of war by force. It is necessary that the victors are superior of the vanquished in intelligence. Only when the conquerors are fully satisfied that the prisoners of war are inferior in intelligence they should be made slaves.

**2. Kind of Treatment to the Slaves**

Aristotle says that it is the duty of the master to be kind human and gentle to the slave. The master should talk to the slave from time to time, give him a piece of advice and create good conditions of life for him. The slaves must be given good food and good clothes. Though they are inferior in intelligence, yet they are useful for the master. They are human beings and must be treated like human beings. Aristotle is of opinion that any master who is guilty of ill-treating the slave deserves to be punished according to law.

**3. Provision for Emancipation**

A slave should not be supposed to be a slave for the whole of his life. If he shows a better conduct, if he gives proof of better reasoning, if he can show evidence of his virtue, he has a right to be emancipated.

### 4. The Master should Use the Slave only to Attain Human Virtue

The master is supposed to use the slave in a way that he (the master) can attain human virtue. The master has no right to use the slave for the purpose of increasing his wealth.[31]

## CRITICISMS

Aristotle has given many arguments to prove that slavery is a natural institution and is useful both for the master and the slave. His arguments, however, are not convincing and are full contradictions and inaccuracies.

We may not the following points of criticism against Aristotle's defence of slavery :

### 1. Aristotle's Theory of Slavery is Opposed to the Democratic and Socialistic Principles of Equality

Aristotle bases his theory on the principle that men are born unequal. He believes that inequality is natural and equality is unnatural. This view is anti-democratic and is against the basic principles of socialism and democracy. Democracy and socialism are based on the principle that all men are equal. To make a large number of people slaves simply on the ground that they are inferior is against the principles of justice and morality. True equality is true morality.

### 2. Aristotle's Theory of Slavery Shows Racial Prejudice

Aristotle's theory of slavery shows that he is prejudiced against other races. Like all Greeks, he believed that the Greeks were superior to other races from the intellectual moral and cultural points of view. Aristotle forgets the basic principle that culture, virtue and intelligence are not the monopoly of any single race. All men all over the world have a right to freedom. By saying that the Greeks were superior to other races, Aristotle was denying the basic and fundamental principles of freedom, justice and equality. It is merely a false prejudice to think that people of one race are superior in intelligence to those of another. There are more intelligent and less intelligent people in all the races.

### 3. Aristotle's Principle of Superiority and Inferiority will Result in Classification of Society into Countless Groups

If Aristotle's principle of the master being superior and the slave being inferior is accepted, the human society will be divided not in two groups—masters and slaves, but in innumerable groups, because each one of us is superior to someone and inferior to some else. The fact is that Aristotle is trying to justify slavery on wrong assumptions.

### 4. It is not Necessary that Physically Strong Men is Unintelligent and an Intelligent Person is Physically Weak

Aristotle's contention that the slaves are physically strong, but weak in intelligence and masters are strong in intelligence but weak is physique is rather artificial and is the result of incomplete and partial observation. There are thousands of examples to prove that physically strong people are very intelligent. A physically weak person is not necessary weak. To make intelligence and physical strength the bases of master-slave relationship is incorrect psychologically and logically.

### Conclusion

There can be no valid, logical, psychological, moral or social reason to justify slavery. Thanks to the efforts of Abraham Lincoin and other pioneers that this unkind institution stands abolished today. By justifying the institution of slavery, Aristotle deprived a large number of human beings of such a precious value as liberty.

## ARISTOTLE'S VIEWS ON FAMILY AND PROPERTY

### Introduction

According to Aristotle, the family is a natural institution. It is the result of two instincts—the instinct of reproduction and the instinct of self-preservation. The union of male and female and the master-slave relationship result in the institution of the family or the household. Aristotle said, family is composite and is bundle of three relationships—master and servant, husband and wife, parent and child. Aristotle said, the family is the first natural institution and the state is the logical development of the family. Therefore, the state is also a natural institution.[32] Aristotle's View About the Family is Different from that of Plato.

Plato wants to abolish the system of private family for the guardians. He thinks that attachment to the family results in greed for property and the rulers cannot perform their duties honestly and effectively if they have families. Plato is of opinion that only communism of wives and children can bring about the unity and harmony in the state. For Plato, the state is a large family.

Aristotle does not accept Plato's view that the family and the state are similar. He points out that the family and the state are different in kind and degree. He gives the following arguments to prove that the family and the state are different institutions.

### 1. There is Only One Kind of Relationship in the State, Whereas there are Manifold Relationships in the Family

While pointing out the difference between the family and the state, Aristotle says that there is only one kind of relationship in the state—the relation between the ruler and the ruled. In the family there are many types of relations. The relation between the head of the household and others is of following types.

**I. Relation Between Husband and Wife.** The husband rules over the wife not as a despotic ruler having unlimited powers, but rules over her as an adviser constitutional limitations.

**II. Relation Between Father and Children.** The father rules over his children not as a despotic ruler, but as a king who is more interested in their good rather than his own good. The father is a well-wisher and benefactor of the children. He does not so much care for his own good as for the good of the children. Therefore, he rules over them.

Here the argument again is that although the child has

soul and mind, but it is in immature form. Children have their own special form of goodness. But since the child is immature, his goodness is obviously not a matter of his relation to his present self, but of his relation to the end. This he will attain on acquiring maturity. His present goodness is also a matter of his relation to the guiding authority of the present which prepares him for that end. Deformed children should not be reared and be exposed and allowed to perish. But this should not be used as a method to keep the population down. If the population is to be kept under check, the size of the family should be limited by law.

**III. The Relation Between Master and Slave.** The master rules over the slaves as over other property like a pure despot, always thinking of his own interest and not of the interest of the slaves.

### 2. The Family Exists for the Satisfaction of Physical Needs, the State Exists for Promoting the Moral Good

Another very important difference, according to Aristotle, between the family and the state is that the family exists only for the satisfaction of physical needs, whereas the state promotes the highest good or the moral good. In other words the state is there for moral good of the individuals. In the state, the individual realises his best personality.

### 3. The State is a Whole, the Family is a Part

According to Aristotle, the state is a whole, the family is a part. The state is a large circle and includes many families and villages. The family is prior in time, the state is prior in thought.

## ARISTOTLE'S VIEWS ABOUT PROPERTY

### Introduction

Aristotle is famous in the history of political thought for his views on property. Whereas Plato abolished property for the guardians, Aristotle attaches great importance to the institution of property and gives a detailed description of methods of acquiring wealth. Infact, his views about wealth getting and wealth—spending have become the guiding principles for writers on political economy.

## ARISTOTLE DOCTRINE OF PROPERTY IS BASED ON WEALTH

### 1. Wealth does not Mean Coined Money

By wealth, Aristotle does not mean coined money. He means only those instruments living and non-living and those objects of possession which are necessary in a household to make good life possible.

### 2. Aristotle Places Limitations on Wealth

Aristotle does not favour abolition of property as Plato does, though for a part of the population, the guardians. Aristotle thinks that property is essential for making good life possible in a household. Aristotle, however, wants limited wealth for the household. To have more than needed is also a vice. The right thing is a middle course. Here Aristotle gives his famous doctrine of the 'Golden Mean'. For example, rashness is an excess and is a vice. Cowardice is a defect and is a vice. Courage stands in the middle and is a virtue.

Similarly, too much wealth is a vice. Not having wealth is a vice. Poverty is an evil because it leads to degeneration and corruption. Having limited wealth which is essential for the needs of the household is an important condition for virtuous and moral life. A hammer must be heavy in order to serve its purpose, but the object of the hammer-maker, will not, therefore, to be make it as heavy as possible. The same function of the hammer which demands weight also sets a limit to the weight required, and the good hammer-maker will observe this limit.

### 3. Aristotle Attaches No High Philosophical Significance to Production of Wealth

Aristotle does not attach any high philosophical significance to the production of wealth. According to him, production of wealth is the lowest function of the household. According to

Aristotle, "The purpose of the household management is to make the members of the family virtuous rather than rich".

**Defence of Private Property**

Aristotle gives many arguments to justify and defend the institution of property. Some of these arguments are given below :

1. **Private property gives incentive to the individual and leads to the progress of society.**

Aristotle is of opinion that the individual gets an incentive to work harder when he knows that the result of his hard labour will be acquisition of property. When everyone works harder and harder because of this incentive there is the progress of society as a whole. Property leads to advancement of society in all directions. It is a great motivating force. Society marches towards civilization and progress because of the institution of private property.

2. **Possession of wealth gives pleasure.**

According to Aristotle, possession of wealth gives pleasure to its holder. Wealth is a great source of happiness. It gives rise to a feeling of self love and self respect. Wealth gives a feeling of self-importance to its possessor. According to Aristotle, there is no selfishness in the possession of wealth. Almost all men are desirous of possessing wealth because it is a source of happiness. One can appreciate this point by understanding that a person living in his own house is far happier than a tenant. Property is a mirror through which one can see one's personality. In others words, a man can judge his personality by assessment of the property acquired by him.

3. **According to Aristotle, private property is an instrument of good life.**

Aristotle believes that private property is a very important instrument of good life. It is the means for the development of human personality. Righteous and virtuous life is possible only for those who have property. The virtues of charity, liberality, hospitality and generosity cannot be practiced by propertyless people. Those who have nothing to give cannot help the needy and the deserving. Only people having property can be generous, liberal, hospitable and charitable in actual practice, private property is the foundation of righteous and noble life.[33]

**4. According to Aristotle, the institution of private property is good because it has been handed over to us through ages.**

Aristotle believes that the institution of private property is useful and good because it has come down to us through ages. Since it has continued to exist all these times, it is apparent that it is a very useful, important and noble institution. Had the institution of private property been harmful and dangerous, it would have been abolished. The fact of its continuation is a proof of its usefulness.

**5. Property encourages civic virtues and develops a sense of responsibility.**

According to Aristotle, the person who does not possess private property cannot make any contribution to the development of the state. A propertyless person cannot be the right type of a citizen. He cannot have civic virtues. Those who have property have a better sense of civic responsibility than those who do not possess it. People who have property are interested in the state affairs because they depend upon the state for protection of their property. For this reasons, Aristotle gives the right of citizenship only to those who have property. Property, according to Aristotle is an essential condition of citizenship.

**6. Experience in management of private property enables the individual to manage the state affairs.**

Aristotle thinks that the holders of private property acquires an experience in management. Experience in the management of their property gives them a sufficient training in managing the state-affairs. Participation in the state affairs is the right of those who own property.

## METHODS OF ACQUIRING WEALTH

Economics he treats as separate from the auxiliary to social life. Property is an important element in the family for it is impossible to live without means of subsistence and the means of subsistence may produce differences in the ways of life. There are two ways of acquiring the property said Aristotle. These two methods are :

### 1. The Natural Methods

The natural methods of acquiring wealth are those which aim at obtaining necessary provisions for mere subsistence. Natural methods are for the sake of livelihood. The natural method is necessary, desirable and good. All wealth must have limit otherwise, the effort made to acquire it would violate virtue. The proper function of intellect or reason is not to produce money but to give knowledge and wisdom, that of courage to give confidence. The natural way to get wealth for the family is skilful management of house and land.

Aristotle mentions the following natural methods of acquiring wealth. 1. Cattle-raising, 2. Agriculture, 3. Hunting, 4. Fishing, 5. Chase of land animals, 6. Brigandage.

### 2. The Unnatural Methods

Aristotle is of opinion that the unnatural methods of acquiring wealth are those which aim at endless accumulation of wealth and not mere procurement of subsistence. The unnatural method is for the sake of accumulation. This method is undesirable, pernicious and full of injustice. Aristotle mentions the following methods in this list.

**(I) Trade.** Trade whether in the form of barter or in the form of sale for money when pursued with the aim of acquiring heaps of money and making money an end in itself is an unnatural method of acquiring wealth. Wealth earned from the trade is hateful because it is unnatural.

**(II) Lending Money on Interest.** Lending money on interest is an unnatural method of acquiring wealth because the aim of money-lenders is not procure mere subsistence but to increase their money. The most hateful method of earning money is usury because it is unnatural breeding of money out of money.[34]

## ARISTOTLE'S CLASSIFICATION OF THE STATE

### Introduction

In his great book, 'The Politics,' Aristotle discusses the nature, origin, functions and purpose of the state, the functions of the family or household justification of slavery and property. He diseases citizenship in an elaborate manner defines the constitution and discusses the classification of the states. Aristotle's classification of the states, though not applicable in modern times, is still the guiding classification.[35]

All students, teachers and writers of political science must study Aristotle's classification of the states, before studying any other classification. His classification of states is a subject of permanent interest. Aristotle gave this classification of the states after studying in details the constitutions of 158 countries. The constitution of Athens has survived to serve as an illustration. In modern times, we make a distinction between the state, government and the constitution. For Aristotle, there was no distinction between these three. He identifies all these three.

The modern writers, think that government is a person or a group of persons in whose hands the state has given the power to carryout its will. It is thought today that the government is a concrete and the state is abstract, that government is a part and the state is a whole, that government is temporary and the state is permanent. The constitution is defined today as a collection of rules and regulations which are regarded as binding by the government.

Aristotle identifies all the three. For him, the state, government and the constitution are the same. He says, the constitution is infact, government. The essence of the state is the constitution and the state changes its identity when the constitution changes. Aristotle defines the constitution as "the arrangement of magistrates in a state, especially of the highest of all." The constitution is not merely the part of the state. It is the state.

**Bases of Classification**

Aristotle classifies constitutions or governments or states or political systems on two bases.

**1. The End or Purpose Before the Rulers**

For classification of the states or governments or constitutions, Aristotle takes into consideration the end or purpose before the rulers. If the ruler or rulers always think of their interest and ignore the interest of the people, it is a perverted form of government or bad or corrupt form of government. If the ruler or rulers think of the interest of the people and rule for their welfare, the form of government is normal or good or pure.

**2. The Number of the Rulers**

The second basis of Aristotle's classification of the states is the number of the persons in whose hands the power of administration lies. On this basis, he gives the following forms of government.

**I. Rule of One.** If the government is in the hands of one ruler, the form of government is monarchy, when the ruler rules for the welfare of the people. In other words, the normal or pure or good government is monarchy when one ruler rules. If the ruler rules for his own interest and totally ignores the interests of the people, the form of government is tyranny. The corrupt or perverted or bad form of monarchy is tyranny.

**II. Rule of the Few.** If the few rule for the welfare of the people, the form of government is Aristocracy. If they rule in their own interest, the form of government is oligarchy. Aristocracy is the normal or pure or good form of government. Aristocracy is the normal or pure or good form of government. Oligarchy is perverted or corrupt or bad form of government.

**III. Rule of Many.** When the many rule for the common welfare, the form of government is polity. When the may rule in the interest of the poor alone, ignoring the interest of all the others, the form of government is democracy. Polity is the normal or pure or good form of government. Democracy is the perverted or corrupt or bad form of government.

Aristotle says, of forms of government in which on rules, we call that which regards the common interest, kingship or royalty, that in which more than one but not many, rule, aristocracy. But when the citizens at large administer the state for the common interest, the government is called polity. The true forms of government and those in which the one or the few or the many govern with a view to the common interest, but governments which rule with a view to the private interest, whether of the one, or of the few, or of the many, are perversions.

Of the above-mentioned forms, the perversions are as follows : Of Royalty, Tyranny, Of Aristocracy—Oligarchy, Of Polity—Democracy. For tyranny is a kind of monarchy which has in view the interest of the monarch only. Oligarchy has in view the interest of the wealthy; democracy of the needy; none of them the common good of all.[36]

Aristotle's classification of states can be explained in the following tabular form :

**Aristotle's Classification of States**

| Number of Rulers | Pure or normal or good government (in which the rulers rule for the welfare of the people.) | Corrupt or perverted or bad government (in which the rulers rule for their own interest) |
|---|---|---|
| (I) One | Monarchy | Tyranny |
| (II) The Few | Aristocracy | Oligarchy |
| (III) The many | Polity | Democracy |

Monarchy is the best form of government. Tyranny and democracy are the worst.

## REFERENCES

1. A great disciple of a great teacher, Aristotle has rightly been called the father of political science. He made the most

remarkable contribution to political thought. His scientific approach to political problems his inductive method and above all, his intelligent study of 158 constitutions, place him at the top of the list of all political thinkers of the world.

2. Besides Social Sciences, Aristotle also studied natural or pure or physical sciences.
3. Gettel, History of Political Thought, p. 68.
4. Dunning, A History of Political Theories, p. 93.
5. Gettel, History of Political Thought, *op. cit.*, p. 98.
6. M.G. Gupta, History of Political Thought, p. 120.
7. Aristotle, 'Politics', p. 120.
8. Aristotle said, the state is the association of associations.
9. Family is the basic unit of the state says Aristotle.
10. Quoted by Foster, Masters of Political Thought, pp. 155-156.
11. Foster, *op. cit.*, pp. 158-160.
12. Aristotle called the rule of the middle class as the 'Golden Mean'.
13. Sabine, A History of Political Theory, p. 88.
14. Dunning, A History of Political Theories, p. 49.
15. Foster, Masters of Political Thought, p. 122.
16. Aristotle, Politics Book I.
17. Dunning, A History of Political Theories, *op. cit.*, pp. 50-52.
18. Dunning, *op. cit.*, pp. 54-58.
19. Foster, Masters of Political Thought, p. 123.
20. Foster, Masters of Political Thought, *op.cit.*, p. 124.
21. Dunning explains that the poor or the working classes are indeed essential to the state's existence, but this does not constitute them citizens.
22. Aristotle was a realist and the actualists and his ideas are based on the observation of facts.

23. Gettel says, "The frequent changes in the government or the constitution of the Greek cities led Aristotle to devote considerable attention to the subject of revolution."
24. Aristotle said, revolution is not a simple concept, but it is a comprehensive one as it includes changes not only in the political realm, but also social, economic, cultural and educational realms.
25. Revolutions always start in mind. Before actual revolutions take place, there is always a revolution in the minds of men. Men have a strong desire for justice. There is a disturbance, a revolt in their minds against injustice.
26. Dunning, A History of Political Theories, p. 59-64.
27. Dunning, A History of Political Theories, p. 89.
28. Sabine said, 'The slave is a living tool to be kindly used, but still used for the master's good'
29. We can explain this point in the following words of dunning,

    "Men differ from one another in capacity for one or the other of these functions. There are those whose high endowment of reason fits them to command and direct. There are those whose slight endowment fits them only to carry out orders. The former are by nature masters, the latter are by nature slaves.
30. We can say that one of the reasons why Aristotle was in favour of slavery was that the existing conditions in Athens and other Greek city-states had made slavery a social and economic necessity.
31. Aristotle justified slavery on the ground that a slave gives leisure to the master and enables him to develop the moral and intellectual excellence of which he is capable.
32. Quoted by Foster, Masters of Political Thought, p. 132.
33. Dunning, A History of Political Theories, p. 93.
34. Unnatural method is the worst method of acquiring the property said Aristotle.
35. Practically, all those who undertake the task of classifying the states and of constitution making must study Aristotle's

classification of governments and they, will find very valuable and useful hints and guidance for such a formidable task.

36. According to Aristotle, polity is that form of government in which the rulers who are many in number belong to the middle class and rule for the welfare of all. Aristotle is of opinion that polity is the best practicable state.

# 3

# Roman Political Thought
## (Polybius and Cicero)

### Introduction

The contribution of the Romans to political philosophy is not so important as that of the Greeks. The Romans are more famous for their political institutions and legal system than for their political philosophy. Many countries of the west learnt a good deal from the Roman Political Institutions. The legal system of the Romans played a very important part or role in helping other countries to mould their legal systems. The Romans did not make so much contribution to political thought as the Greeks did. The Roman political philosophers, Polybius and Cicero do not occupy that important position in the history of political thought as Plato and Aristotle do. The Romans, however, set very important examples before the world by developing well organized political institutions and their excellent legal system.[1]

Following are the important points of the Roman political thought :

**1. The contribution of the romans to political philosophy is very little. Their political institutions and legal system are very important.**

The Romans did not contributed much to political thought. The Romans were famous for their legal system. They had a well-organized system of political institutions. Though the contribution of the Romans to political philosophy was very little, yet their political institutions and legal system moulded western political institutions and legal systems.

**2. In the beginning Rome was a City State.**

In the beginning, Rome was a city-state. The government of the city-state consisted of the monarch, the Senate and the Assembly. The Senate was only a advisory body.[2] The chief function of the assembly was the election of the king. In the beginning, political rights and powers were in the hands of the aristocratic class—the patricians. The plebeians or the common people were excluded from political rights and political powers. Afterwards, the plebeians also got representation in the government. An additional assembly called Comitia Centuriata was formed. This assembly represented the patricians (the aristocratic people) and the plebians (The common people).

**3. Rome become a republic about 500 B.C.**

Rome became a republic about 500 B.C. The patricians and the plebians formed the citizen-body. There were two consuls in place of the king. The consuls were assisted by the representative of the people—The Tribune. There was always a struggle for political power between the patricians and the plebians. In the later days of the republic, the distinction between the patricians and the plebians practically disappeared and a very important lawmaking body emerged. The Senate which consisted of very experienced and important politicians of the republic continued to function as an advisory body.

**4. Rome an Empire.**

The Emperor Autocratic Ruler. By the end of the 2nd century A.D., Rome became a very big empire. All the powers of the government were in the hands of the emperor. Julius Caesar and Augustus had established military despotism in Rome. It was believed that the people had given power to the emperor for all times. The emperor was worshipped like a God. It was believed that the powers of the emperor was derived from God. When Rome was converted to Christianity, it was believed that the emperor was the agent of God's will on earth.

**5. Roman Ideals.**

Rome which was in the beginning a city-state with a democratic form of government, because a very big empire having an autocratic emperor as the head of the empire. The Greek ideals of democracy, liberty and independence of the city-state were no longer there. In place of these ideals there were these Roman Ideals—Unity, Order, Universal Law and Cosmopoltianism. The Romans derived some of their ideals from the stoics.

**Nature and Special Characteristics of Roman Political Thought**

The Roman political thinkers were not so original in their political thought as the Greeks. They were not so imaginative, as Plato was. None of the Roman writers showed that blending of idealism and realism as Aristotle did. The Roman political thinkers were influenced by Greek political ideas. They were specially indebted to the stoics. Plato and Aristotle did not exercise much influence on their writings.

We may not special features or characteristics of the Roman political thought as follows :

**1. According to the Romans, the state was essential and was at the same time natural.**

The Roman political, thinkers were of opinion that the state was essential and was at the same time natural. The state according to them was a legal personality. It had rights and duties. The individual also had his rights and duties. The main functions of the state was the protection of the rights of the individual.

**2. The Roman idea about the relation between the state and the individual was different from that of the greek.**

The Roman idea about the relation between the state and the individual was different from tat of the Greeks. The Greek philosophers did not separate the individual from the state. Plato thought that the individual was the state in little. The state was individual write large. The individual had no existence apart from the state. The Romans on the other hand, separated the individual from the state. They thought that the individual and the state were two separate legal personalities, each having rights and duties.

**3. The Romans created an elaborate and comprehensive system of law.**

The Roman's created an elaborate and comprehensive system of law on the basis of this concept of the relation between the state and the indvidual. The greatest contribution of the Romans was a well-defined well-arranged, well-organized, elaborate and comprehensive legal system.

The Romans gave three types of laws :

*(a)* The law regulating the property and family rights of the Roman citizens. This was the Civil Law (Jus Civile) regulating the relations of the Roman citizens.

*(b)* The law which regulated the relations between the Roman citizens and subjects of the Roman empire. This was the Law of Nations. (Jus Centium).

*(c)* The law of nature was borrowed by the Romans from the stoics. According to the law, all men were equal. The Romans called this law Jus Natural. Slavery could be justified only by the Low of Nations, and not by civil law and Law of Nature.

**4. The Roman thinkers thought that the rulers derived sovereignty from the people.**

The Roman lawyers and political thinkers thought that the ruler had legal sovereignty. Whether the ruler was the king or the consul or the dictator, legal sovereignty was with him. The ruler derived the legal sovereignty from the people. The people were the real holders of political power. In Republican Rome, people actually wielded great authority. The republic was governed by the representatives of the people.

**5. The Romans were the originators of the idea of a contract between the people and the emperor the idea of a governmental contract.**

As long as there was the republican system of government in Rome, there was no difficulty in the idea of political sovereignty being with the people. In the days of the emperor this idea appeared to be rather paradoxical. How could it be assumed that the people were the holders of political sovereignty when the emperor's will was law? The Roman lawyers and political thinkers came forward with a new idea. This was the idea of the contract between the people and the emperor. The Roman thinkers said that the people had agreed to be commanded by the emperor. These thinkers did not mention any specific time when the people transferred to the emperor the right to command. People had given powers to the emperor forever and could never take those powers back. This was the governmental contract. The emperor was considered to be absolute because people had given him absolute powers. The emperor's will was law.[3]

**6. In the days of the roman emperor, some people believed that the emperor had divine authority to rule over them.**

It was believed by some people during the days of the Roman emperors that the emperors derived their powers from God. The emperor was worshipped like a God. When Rome was converted to Christianity, it was believed that the Emperor was "the agent of God's will on earth."

The Romans did not possess that philosophical, imaginative and idealistic attitude of the mind as the Greeks possessed. The attitude of the Romans was legal and practical. Their contribution to political thought was not very great, but they made significant and useful contribution by their well-defined legal system and systematically evolved political institutions. The Romans contributed to the world the concept of popular sovereignty, the idea of the contractual basis of the government. The concept of International Law was developed from their concept of the Law of Nations (Jus Gentium). The Romans also gave to the world the idea of private rights of the individual and the legal personality of the state and the individual. Many writers haved based their theories of sovereignty on the ideas of the Romans. The Romans freed laws from religion and morality and gave them a secular and positive shape. The Romans popularized the stoic idea of Cosmopolitanism.[4]

**Conclusion**

The Romans did not show any striking originality in their political thought. They did not enrich the stock of world's political ideas. Their remarkable contributions were their legal system and their political institutions.

The above-mentioned contributions of the Romans were their enduring contributions. Some of the Roman ideas haunted the middle ages. We must not forget that the Romans were the borrowers of ideas from the Greek stoics. They were transmitters of ideas which they had borrowed. They did not make any remarkable original contribution to political thought.

## POLYBIUS

## (204 B.C.—122 B.C.)

**Introduction**

Polybius is the most important Greek historian and he lived to be 80 and to die of a fall from his horse. He was an active shrewd men. From boyhood he had been among politicians, men of affairs, and military generals. He had acquired a great knowledge of military science and strategy. He had kept is ears and eyes open and he heard fateful accounts of events and witnessed great changes. From his days of youth, he was not so much interested in what happened and as 'why' it happened. He is an active citizen in the study of history.[5] It is an article of his faith. He combined a sharp mind, a variety and profound experience acquired from wide contacts with men and material. He had travelled widely and had a personal knowledge of battles fought and of the men who had participated there in. He had a deep respect for the truth.

**Life and Works**

Polybius was a Greek by birth. When the Romans conquered Macedonia, he was taken as a prisoner to Rome along with other Greek prisoners. He was kept as a political hostage in Rome for seventeen (17) years. The Roman government sent him on several missions to Greece. While Polybius was in Rome, he acquainted himself with the Roman constitution and the Roman statesmen.

He became leading light of the group of statesmen. He was moderate and favoured a policy of a negative attitude towards Rome. He was one of the hostages of Rome. Here they all lived like distinguished guests either than as prisoners. In Rome Polybius had the great fortune of cultivating the friendship of younger 'scipio' whom he accompanied on many of his campaigns. He also acquired a good knowledge of the Latin tongue. The Romans recognized his shrewdness, political wisdom, experience, worth and ability. He was appointed as a mediator to effect conciliation between Rome and the Achaeans. He spent the last years of his life in leisure, travel, collection of material, and pursuit of knowledge under the patronage of scipio. He roused Rome to dominant position. His work in 40 books of which only the first five survive entire, though there are fragments of most of the others.

It is in the part of the book that luckily survives, that we have the political philosophy of Polybius. Polybius denied that the human affairs were governed by destiny or by providence or ruled by chance or accident. Strange chances may sometimes lead to stronger chances, but it was different with Rome. Polybius gives the answer that Rome's domination was due to the fact that she had a sound constitution, she did not neglect her military affairs, and managed them well, the citizens were honest.[6]

As a historian, Polybius is plain and practical, matter of fact and impartial in his observation of events, his aim being accuracy rather than expression of admiration. He kept his emotions to himself. Though consistently loyal to his native Greece, he was inspired throughout by a sense of the invisible strength of the Roman power, and the nobility and greatness of Roman character and institutions.

## POLITICAL IDEAS

He was a political philosopher, his observation are verbose and some what banal. His political thought finds a place in the VIth book of his history. He touches the origin of the state, the forms of government, the cycle of political changes and the theory of

'Mixed Government' based on separation of powers and the checks and balances of which Roman constitution, was the supreme example. Polybius was originally a Greek. He was brought as a prisoner to Rome when the Romans conquered Macedonia. He was kept as a political hostage in Rome for 17 years. Polybius wrote history of Rome to explain the causes of Rome's rise to power and the secret of her control over her vast territories.[7]

Polybius was impressed by the Roman constitution. He wrote at a time when Rome had a 'Republican form of government.' He observed the Roman constitution carefully and impartially and was much impressed by it. He came to the conclusion that the Romans were successful in safeguarding their country from decay, because they had introduced a system of 'Check and balances' in their constitution. The Romans had a stable form of government because only they had mixed constitution—blending together the best elements of monarchy, aristocracy and democracy. Polybius is famous for his classification of governments.

## ORIGIN OF THE STATE

Polybius said, mutual interest urged men to unite under the leadership of one person. Before the civil society, there is neither law nor justice, neither virtue nor goodness. It is only when family ties develop, that social relations could be possible. Sex instinct leads to paining and mating. Children are born and families begin to expand. Children becomes adults after attaining maturity. Some of them may become ungrateful to their parents and refuse to return kindness to kindness. Some of them injure their parents by hard and harsh words. He said, 'duty must be done.' People then round the despot and tend to follow and obey him. There is no longer a fear of violence. Life becomes regulated. The despot is no longer issues commands or laws which are instinctively carried out. Despotism now acquires legitimacy and the despot become a king. The state has now come into existence.

Thus, according to Polybius, the origin of the state lies in the principles of man's instinct of self-preservation. Mutual interdependence, utility and reason and the earliest form of despotism which later came to be transformed into kingship. The king though physically, intellectually, and morally superior to the rest, always identified himself with the subjects. His power becomes dynastic and hereditary. The only sanction of kingship becomes the accident of birth. Further, personal comfort is expanded into luxury. Appetite now reign supreme. Their dress becomes gorgeous. They get fond of elaborate luxuries of the table. They began to keep mistresses and concubines. There is no longer that easy intimacy between them and their subjects. They now become unnatural. The ruler, therefore, begins to be hated by the subjects who now becomes jealous and resentful discontent grows. The king becomes a tyranny and the people now plan his over-throw, and plots begin to be formed against the government. Aristocracy ends in oligarchy. But when their son succeed them, they also got corrupt. So the constitution changed from oligarchy to democracy.

However, with the passage of the time people's rule also generates. Rivalries, bickering and a race for power an the self seizes the state. Bribery and negotism become the order of the day. Might becomes right culture decays, civilization perishes. Once strong master emerges and becomes a despot. Hence, Polybius think interims of change.

## FORMS OR CLASSIFICATION OF GOVERNMENTS

Polybius was originally a Greek. He borrowed ideas from Plato and Aristotle to give his classification of governments. His list of pure forms of government is the same as that of Plato. Polybius also gave a perverted form corresponding to each of these pure forms. The basis of classification is three fold : 1. Number, 2. Nature of acceptance of authority, 3. End.

A brief account of Polybius classification governments is given below :

### 1. Monarchy

If the government is run by one men and his rule is accepted voluntarily, and he rules in common interest, it is Monarchy or Kingship. According to Polybius monarchy is the earliest form of government. People learnt the value of the monarch's authority by reason and experience and offered him willing obedience.

**2. Corrupted form of Monarchy—Tyranny**

The perverted form of monarchy is tyranny. Polybius pointed out that monarchy degenerated into tyranny. When the monarch began to exercise his powers in a cruel, unjust and arbitrary way, monarchy was perverted into tyranny—the corrupted form of monarchy. Thus, monarchy's perverted form is tyranny. It is a rule based on fear and force. It is a government not in common interest, but only in the interest of the tyrant.

**3. Aristocracy**

If the government is in the hands of few and their rule commands voluntarily acceptance and it is in common interest, it is Aristocracy. The tyrant was overthrow and there emerged Aristocracy under the leadership of a few wise and distinguished people.

**4. Oligarchy**

Aristocracy had in it germs of its own weaknesses. When men power become the oppressors of the people, the perverted form of Aristocracy appeared on the scene. The perverted form of Aristocracy was oligarchy. Oligarchy is degenerated form of Aristocracy.

**5. Democracy**

People protested against these oppressing oligarchs and established the government of the people for the interest of all. This forms of government was democracy. If the government is in the hands of many (people) whose authority is based on voluntary acceptance, which rules in the interest of the whole people, it is democracy.

**6. Mob-rule (Mobocracy)**

Democracy also failed because the ignorant masses were

corrupted by the wealthy. There was no justice. Injustice made people discontented. The result was the mob-rule-Mobocracy. The perversion of democracy is Mobocracy.

### The Cycle Started Again

When the mob-rule took the place of democracy, some bold leader again computered power and the cycle started a fresh. Therefore Polybius suggested 'Mixed' forms of government with checks and balances.[9]

According to Polybius the pure forms of government were : 1. Monarchy, 2. Aristocracy, 3. Democracy.

The perverted or corrupted or degenerated forms of government were : 1. Tyranny, 2. Oligarchy, 3. Mob-rule (Mobocracy or Ochlocracy).

Polybius also suggested or says that a government is good or bad according as it produces citizens of good or bad moral character.

## BEST FORM OF GOVERNMENT

According to Polybius, the best form of government in neither Monarchy nor Aristocracy nor Democracy, because in every one of them power flows from top to bottom which is one way traffic. There exists a gulf or gap between the rulers and the ruled. The best constitution, therefore, is that which partakes of all these three elements centralized rule of the monarchy, decentralized principle of Aristocracy and broad base of democracy. That would ensure the flow down of power from top to bottom and flow up of authority from the base to the top. If all these elements are three elements are combined, they would check and balance each other and the harmony and proportion of the entire state would be maintained. The best example that Polybius given is that of Rome which combined all the three elements into a state of equilibrium : 1. The consuls represented monarchy, 2. The senate represented Aristocracy, 3. The assembly represented democracy.

The balance was so nice and their respective share of power

in the whole state had been regulated with such a scrupulous regard to equality and equilibrium, one should not say certainly whether it was a whole aristocracy or democracy or despotism. Every element kept the other under restraint, and no single element could raises its head to get drunk with power. None of the organs of the government could afford to interfere or thwart the working of the other. The consuls were the principal executive, senate controlled money, public works, investigation of crimes, foreign relations and in the absence of the consuls. It was a real ruler. The people were the fountain of honour and justice. They were final tribunal for settlement of cases. The consuls were important and so was the senate. But there was a very important role for the people to play. The people then are the only court to decide matters of life and death. People bestow offices on the deserving which are the most honourable rewards of virtue. It has the absolute power of passing the laws. They deliberate on the question of war and peace. When provisional terms are made for alliance, suspension of hostilities or treaties. It is the people who ratify them or the reverse. The considerations again would lead one to say that the chief power in the state was the people and the constitution was a democracy.

Thus, Polybius argues that in the Roman system, there was a clear division of power between the three organs of government or three parts of the state. But they could never run into opposite directions. They deepened upon each other and none of them could function without each others support. The consuls depended upon the Senate for sanction of money, without which they could not fight the wars, for their election which was yearly and for numerous other things. They also depended upon the people who alone could ratify treaties and to whom they had to given account of their administration at the end of their term.

Similarly, senate is also possesses immense powers. But it was also controlled by the people. The decrees of the Senate awarding death sentences had to be ratified by the people. The people could also curtail or enhance the privileges of the

Senators. The Senate and consults protected the life. The Senate appointed judges who tried serious charges against the citizens. The consuls during emergencies, became all powerful and exercised absolute authority.

### Conclusion

Polybius was the father of Roman political thought. Polybius though that the best way to have a stable form of government was to combine the best elements of each of these forms. Since each one of these forms had in it the seeds of degeneration and downfall, Polybius suggested a combination of the best elements and a system of checks and balances. He saw in republican Rome the best example of the stable form of government. The consuls represented the monarchical idea. The Senate represented the aristocratic elements. The assembly stood for democratic idea. Polybius was the first writer to suggest a system of combination of different elements in the state. He was the first to suggest a system of checks and balances.

Polybius idea influenced many other writers of political thought. He was the forerunner of the French Philosopher Montesquieu who gave the theory of separation of powers in his book the 'Spirt of Laws. The framers of the American constitution applied this idea. Infact, Polybius idea of the system of checks and balances has become a very important idea in political thought.

## CICERO
## 106 B.C.—43 B.C.

### Life and Works

Cicero was a politician, historian, orator, philosopher, poet, political thinker, critic, moralist, and a advocate. Thus, he is a multi-faceted personality.[10] Cicero was a very famous Roman orator. He introduced Stoic philosophy in Rome. He was not only a great lawyer. He expressed his ideas in a very impressive style. There was not much originality in his political thought. He borrowed most of his ideas from Plato, Polybius and the Stoics. Cicero was born in 106 B.C. and died in 43 B.C. Born at

Arpinum, a small town in the volscan hills about 60 miles South-East of Rome. He lived in the days of the decline of the Roman Republic. He saw the civil war between the Patricians (the wealthy people) and the Plebians (the common people). Cicero and his brother received education in Rome. Cicero was first appeared as an advocate in 81 B.C. He was a Roman famous lawyer or advocate.

Meanwhile, he married a women of noble birth, Terentia who bore him two children a daughter Tullia and a son Marcus whose indolent and extravagant habits caused him worry and concern. In 66 B.C. he made his first important political speech. He set out a political career in which after holding several offices with distinction, he was elected consul for 63 B.C.

As a lawyer and a scholar of antiquity, he was passionately attached to the ancient constitution. His political ideal was the natural outcome of his temperament education. He said middle class form of government is the best. The senate authority should be vigorous, and public spirited. It elects magistrates and passed the laws. In 46 B.C. he divorced his wife, and in 45 B.C. he lost his beloved daughter Tullia. Pompey was murdered in 45 B.C. and Caesar in 44 B.C.

Cicero was killed by Antony's troops and his head and right hand were nailed to the rostra or public platform where he had be accustomed to speak against Antony.

Cicero also saw the days of Caesar's supreme power.[11] He was in favour of the republican form of government. He wanted the restoration of the mixed constitution. He was against autocratic rule and was opposed to Caeser's rise to power. He was a supporter of the revival of the old Roman institutions, traditions and virtues.

**His Works**

Cicero expressed his thoughts in three books :

1. The Republica (The Republic)
2. De-Legibus (The laws)

3. De-Officis (The Offices)

As a political thinker Cicero deducted his political ideas from Plato, Aristotle, Polybius. Cicero rejected democracy, oligarchy, monarch (the best of the three) in favour of a mixed constitution. His method was both inductive and deductive. His theory of knowledge, justice, law are largely deductive. He says no man should neglect politics or business of government. His argument is that the wise the scholarly and virtuous men cannot or ought not to participate in political affairs. Political affairs is not only a stupid but highly immoral.[12]

## INFLUENCES IN CICERO

### Introduction

Cicero was a famous Roman orator and lawyer. He lived in the days of the decline of the republic. He saw the civil war between the wealthy Romans and the common people—the patricians and the plebians. He saw Caesar's rise to power and was against it. He was in favour of revival of republican form of government. There is not much originality in his thoughts. He borrowed his ideas from the Stoics, Plato and Polybius. Cicero's most famous book is De-Republica. (The Republic).

Cicero was not a original philosopher. He borrowed his ideas from other philosophers and presented those ideas in an impressive style. In order to understand Cicero's political philosophy, it is important to know the sources of his philosophy or the influences on his philosophy or his indebtedness to other philosophers.

A brief account of influences on Cicero's political thought is given below :

### 1. Cicero Borrowed His Idea of Justice from Plato's Republic

Cicero wrote his De Republica (The Republic) in the form of a dialogue following the style of Plato. Cicero himself, his brother, his friends and some other Romans are participants in this dialogue. The main theme in Cicero's Republic is justice in the Ideal State, as it is the main theme in Plato's Republic. Cicero was a Platonist. His ambition was to write a master-piece in Latin as Plato had written his great treatise, the Republic in Greek.

**2. Cicero Borrowed His Ideas from Polybius**

Cicero who lived almost a hundred years after Polybius was greatly impressed by his ideas and borrowed from him. Like Polybius, Cicero also thought that the Republican form of government the mixed constitution was the best and most suitable for Rome. Cicero also based his classification of government on Polybius classification.

**3. The Stoic Philosophy had a Marked Influence on Cicero**

Cicero was the first famous Roman thinker to support and popularise stoic ideas. From the stoic philosophers, he borrowed the idea of law of nature and also the following ideas : *(a)* Cosmopolitanism, *(b)* Universal Brotherhood, *(c)* World Citizenship.

**4. Influence of His Times**

Cicero lived during the days of the decline of Roman Republic. He saw the civil war between the patricians (the wealthy class) and the plebians (the common people). He saw Caesar's rise to power. The main object of Cicero's writings was to teach the Romans that the republican form of government was the best and most suitable for Rome. He wanted his countrymen to revive republicanism, old Roman institutions and traditions.

## LEADING POLITICAL IDEAS

A brief account of Cicero's political ideas is given below :

Cicero's method was both inductive and deductive. His theory of knowledge, justice, law are largely deductive. He says no men should neglect politics or business of government. His argument is that the wise, the scholarly and virtuous men cannot and ought not to participate in political affairs. Political affairs is not only a stupid but highly immoral.

**1. Doctrine of Natural Law**

Natural law is independent and positive law. It denotes rights or justice held to be common to all mankind. It is based on the observation of the city-states subordination of women to men, of slaves to citizens, the children to parents and of barbarians to hellenes.

He argued that natural law is the true law, right reason, diffused in all men, constant and everlasting. Men in respect of foresight, intelligence, memory, prudence is different from animals and rest of the creation. The source of these attributes is reason which man shares with God. Men unites with God and that is why men alone acknowledge of god. Reason gives birth to virtue. Virtue is nothing but nature fully grown. Nature has given men all the conditions for his fullest development. Men alone can speak through words and can have human intercourse. He alone therefore, has reason. He is thus crown of species. All men are equal. Men discuss problems, comes to conclusions. Evey men has the same senses. All men attain to virtue. He established social equality. All men are alike, all races of men must also be alike. Racial differences are based on ignorance. In natural law you speak racial equality and not racial conflict. The whole human race is one.

The natural law is the basis of civilized society. It urges equality giving each his due. All laws of the state must be in conformity with natural law. The magistrates therefore symbolize the law. Cicero says laws governs the magistrates, so the magistrates governs the people. Magistrates is speaking law and the law is the silent magistrate. The natural law is therefore, unchangeable, immutable, eternal and universal. God is the author of this law, its interpreter and its sponsor.

**2. Law of Nature**

Cicero borrowed his idea of the law of nature from the Stoics. The law of nature is applicable to the entire universe. It is the only true law. This law is eternal and cannot be changed. It is the only true law. This law is eternal and cannot be changed. All human beings must follow it. Even inanimate objects and animals are controlled by this law. According to Cicero, the law of nature is right reason. There is uniformity in the law. The law of nature is unchanging, universal application and ever lasting the law governs all inanimate objects. It governs all animates. It controls all human beings. Necessity compels in animate objects to obey this law. Animals obey this law by instincts and men are guided to obey it.

### 3. Natural Equality

Cicero borrows the idea of natural equality of men from the stoics. He does not accept Plato's and Aristotle's idea of inequality among men. All men are equal because, they have reason. All human beings of all races under proper guidance can attain to virtue. Cicero does not accept Aristotle's justification of slavery. Slaves are not a part of property. They should be treated justly. They also have an independent personality of their own.

### 4. Cicero's Conception of the State

According to Cicero, the state is not the artificial creation. Cicero, is of opinion that the state was not created by men for self-sufficient. It is the result of law of nature which governs the entire universe. This law of nature gives social instinct to man. The state is the result of social instinct. It is natural for men to live in one state or the other. According to Cicero, the state is a partnership in law. Cicero thinks that the state is a rational institution. It is a desirable institution.[13]

Cicero believes that partnership in state business is the highest function for men. This is the realisation of his highest ambition.

### 5. Cicero's Classification of Government

For his classification of governments Cicero borrows ideas from the Greek philosophers Plato, and Aristotle. He is also indebted to Polybius for his classification of governments.

Cicero classifies governments into Monarchy, Aristocracy, and Democracy. He points out that each of these forms has merits and demerits and carries with it the dangers of decay and revolution. Cicero believes that Monarchy is the best form of government. The second best form of government according to him is Aristocracy and democracy is 'the least' desirable form of government. Cicero is in favour of a republican form of government—a mixed constitution having a system of checks and balances. He says, best government is mixed. He prefer a mixed form.

**6. Cicero's Philosophy is Pragmatic**

Cicero's philosophy is pragmatic also.[14] He believes that the same law of nature binds men together all over the world and they become citizens of the world. Cicero preached to the Romans that they were united by partnership in Roman law.

**7. Cicero Preacher Stoic Ideals**

Cicero was greatly influenced by the stoic philosophy. He preserved and preached stoic ideas—universal brotherhood, equality of men, low of nature, world citizenship, public service, humanity, sympathy and kindness.

## CICERO'S CONTRIBUTION

Cicero occupies a very important and honorable place among political thinkers. Though not an original thinker, yet he presents his ideas in an impressive style. We may note his contributions briefly.

In his lifetime Cicero was one of the most dominating influences on roman politics and thought. Cicero's influence immediately operative on his own and succeeding generations. He was a humanist deeply influenced by the French revolution. His works were extensively read and quoted throughout the middle ages. Such words as quality, individual, vacuum, moral, property, induction, definition element, notion, infinity, comprehension, appetite etc. We all owe to Cicero. Cicero who taught us how to think.

He preserved and preached the stoic ideas of the unity of the human race, equality of men, justice, benevolence, love, tolerance and charity towards all fellow-beings. He preached patriotism, high ideals and noble fraditions and virtues among the Romans. Cicero's ideas influenced Church fathers like St. Augustine. The above mentioned contributions of the Cicero were enduring contributions.

## REFERENCES

1. Sabine, A History of Political Theory, p.175.
2. The Roman had the power to accept or reflect the political decisions made by the popular Assembly.
3. The Roman Emperor exercised full powers over the Roman people. People believed that disobedience to the emperor means disobedience to God.
4. Roman's contributed a lot in terms of legal system and the international law.
5. Polybius was an active student of history. He was interested in the study of Rome and the Roman History.
6. Rome was very strong in defense forces, and Romes considered other Nations as 'vassals'. They purchased the friendship of other nations by giving subsidies or favours or concessions. Aid is better than trade was the Roman foreign policy.
7. Seneca, A History of Political Theory, p. 175. Seneca's view is different from that of Polybius who thinks that participation in state business is the highest function for man and is the fulfilment of his highest aspiration. Seneca wrote a time when the Romans had fallen from high qualities in their character. There was corruption. There was degeneration. There was a despotic rule.
8. During the days of Polybius, bribery, corruption and nepotism was rampant. All these are the order of the day.
9. According to Polybius, the Roman constitution was the best because it was a 'mixed' constitution and combined the best elements of monarchy, Aristocracy and Democracy.
10. Foster, Masters of Political Thought, pp. 180-81.
11. Caesar was a Roman dictator. He was an autocrat and despot.

12. Cicero was against the intelligent people to participate in politics because he considered politics is a dirty game, which the gentlemen should not play.
13. The state according to Cicero is the result of the law of nature, which planted social instinct in man.
14. There is an element of pragmatism in Cicero's political philosophy.

# 4

# Political Thought of the Middle Ages

In the middle ages, there was an order of society, it was also an order of thought. The method of debate represented a contention between two contrasting or opposition forces. In owl and nightingale the two birds berate each other and praise themselves, but essentially are used to represent the two different points of view. The owl is the utilitarian, who boasts that he catches rats, but the nightingale is an aesthete who cheers men by his own song. Allegory was doubly used.[1]

Both feudalism and the church were among the major sources of the medieval political thought, *i.e.* the economic and political order. Feudalism meant the virtual disintegration of the state, for the state no longer acted as a whole but in semi-dependent parts. Obedience is to landownership. There was a great impact of the Church on political thought.

## CONTROVERSY BETWEEN CHURCH AND THE STATE

### The Papal Supremacy (The Church)

The argument of this theory is that Church was the sun the state only the moon. The Church was the soul, the state only the body. It wields the swords of justice, the state is the sword of order. The Church is the custodian of the spiritual authority which is superior to the secular authority of the state. The Church is gold the state is merely a lead. The state stands for humility (virtue). The state for arrogance (vice). The saints can bring the dead of life. The state can only take a man from life to death. The Church stands for saviour, the state stands for destruction. The Church men were sinless, the princes and laymen are sinful. It was the duty of the state to protect the

Church. The kings are not therefore, directly responsible to the people. They are responsible to him through the Church. The unholy kings can be deposed by the priests who sit on the throne of God. God sends his messengers to the Church to punish bad unjust and heretical rulers. Jesus had given a clear injunction to Peter "Feed my sheep". Which means that the priests had jurisdiction over the kings. The papal authority was supreme and that the state was subordinate to it. The Church was the right hand, the state, left.

## THE IMPERIAL THEORY THE (STATE)

The imperial theorists argued the independence of the state from the control of the Church. If the Christ had two swords—that for the Church and for the state. It clearly means that the state was the divine as the Church. The rulers were no longer less important than priests. This responsibility could not be to any institution but directly to God. If they sin, they would be punished in life hereafter. If they are cruel or unjust it is only because god willed it so. They should be treated as instruments of the divine will to inflict cruel punishment on the sinners. Everyone must obey the royal commands. All power, it was contended on the authority of Pauline in junctions flows from God and any one who resists power, resists god's will. If the Church was universal, so was the Empire. The analogy of the sun and the moon, the body and the soul the right hand and the left hand are mere metaphors which explain nothing as for as the nature of the state is concerned.

## SALIENT FEATURES OF MEDIEVAL POLITICAL THOUGHT

The middle ages were essentially unpolitical. There was a controversy between the temporal and spiritual power. In other words, it was a controversy between the state and the Church. It has also been said that the middle ages were most unscientific, and uncritical. Medieval political thought was autocratic, authoritarian, dogmatic and unprogressive.[3] If these phrases mean that there was no political thought in the middle ages, their use is unfortunate. Still the philosophy of the middle ages was comprehensive and voluminous, though ill-expressed. M. Bloch said that the middle ages were essentially traditionalist. Every age is traditionalist in some ways, for the tradition of any group—its custom controls its life. But it does not arrest evolution or thinking and it does not exclude fresh ideas.

The middle ages philosophy combine in its philosophy the essential aims and methods of Islam, Judaism, Christianity, the Roman Law, Customs and beliefs. All these three religions were monotheistic. All three believed in incarnations and revelation of God's will in the scriptures. Tradition was of course, held in great esteem, but it does not make the middle ages servile or obscurantist.

It would be more correct to say that the hallmark of medieval thought was its other worldliness. Dante, Aquinas gave importance to moral, natural, and customary law. Aristotle's influence on the middle ages were very great. His influence is not only with regard to logic but also in respect of his political theories and meta physics. He supplied the theory of the nature which was needed to supplement the Church theory of grace. Plato's idealism was working constantly in the background. The Roman's affected not only the medieval law, but also their moral and political ideals. Aquinas followed that Church is good and moral. The Church accepted the Roman principle.

The middle ages supplied the whole argument for monarchy—both speculative and practical. Aquinas made a profound statement, the monarch is the public person for the common good. John Salisbury called the monarch as the representative of his people, bearing their person.

Thus, seen, middle ages were extremely rich in respect of growth of political theory. True, the moddle ages were marked by controversies and even petty quarrels and disfigured by inquisitions. But no age is free from such blemishes.[4] We have to judge the characteristics of Medieval Political thought interms of political institutions and political treatises. None can deny that feudalism gave birth to the notions of loyalty based on contract.

The medieval thinkers did achieve a synthesis between metaphysics and theology and between the claims of human personality and those of the larger systems within which man lives his life. The solutions offered by them were not final.[5]

## REFERENCES

1. Owl is a sign of bad image, where as nightingale bird is beautiful and it is having good qualities and it attracts the people by its melodious songs. It is a sign of goodness.
2. Feudalism means the rule of the land holders or the owners of the land.
3. Foster, History of Political Theories, pp. 45-48.
4. No age is free from good and bad practices.
5. M.G. Gupta, History of Political Thought, pp. 140-150.

# 5

# Saint Augustine
## (354 A.D.—430 A.D.)

### Life and Works

St. Augustine was born in 354 A.D. at Tagaste, a small town in North Africa. His mother Momica was a Catholic whose chief concern and anxiety was the spiritual welfare of her son, but his father Patricius was a pagan whose passion was that his son should receive the best available education. Augustine was therefore sent to neighbouring city Carthage due to poverty. He study with the help of a wealthy family friend Romanianus. Augustine read with great care the works of Cicero and vergil and at the age of 20, he returned home as a teacher of rhetoric which at that time was a craze. He said life as a conflict between the independent powers of light and darkness.[1]

Augustine was a pagan in his youth. He was a brilliant student at Carthage. When he was 33, he adopted the Christian faith. In 395 A.D. he was made the Bishop of Hippo in North Africa. He died in 430 A.D. The Manichanean system, however, disappointed Augustine whose basic questions could not be answered satisfactorily by its experts or exponents. He became disillusioned and was tending to be an agnostic. He taught for sometime at Tagaste and Carthage, he was troubled by the lack of discipline in the African schools and in 383 he set up for Italy. He went first to Rome, Milan, where his mother joined him and where he came strongly under the influence of St. Ambrose, the city's learned eloquent bishop. His prejudice against Christianity was shaken but he still retained the materialistic propositions of the Machiavellian system. He was searching for the being of God, and for the nature and origin and origin of evil.[2]

At this age or stage, he became in contact with the tenets of Neo-Platonism. According to this system, evil is the least real of all things being simply the privation or absence of the good. The inword in good and superior to the outward which is bad. To reach the good which is the real we must return into outselves. That is how he was transformed from a near agnostic into a firm theist. He also claimed to have a mystical experience of the changeless light. God is that light, evil is darkness. But unlike Machiavelli, Augustine now believed neither light nor (God) darkness is a material substance. The changeless light (God) is pure spiritual being and evil is non-existent, a non-entity for, darkness is but the absence of light. Neoplatonic and Manichanean both systems had taught Augustine that the way to return to god is by escaping from the body. Now, he interpreted it to mean escape from sex.

In 386 he was converted and baptized during the Easter-week of the following year. Thus, his curiosity first roused by Cicero's Hortensius was finally satisfied. Augustine now Christian and his mothers fondest hopes had been realised. His mother fell ill in ostia, the port of Rome where she died while waiting to embark. Augustine was left done and he became to tagaste where he spent sometime in theological studies. In 391 he moved to Hippo, a city on a coast about 40 miles to the North, where he was ordained as a priest the same year. He remained at Hippo until his death in 430.

## WORKS AND POLITICAL PHILOSOPHY OF ST. AUGUSTINE

### Introduction

### 1. St. Augustine, a learned and forceful writer

St. Augustine was a very powerful writer. He had acquired vast learning of ancient times. It was through him that a valuable treasure of learning was transmitted to the middle age.[3]

**2. His Works**

St. Augustine was a great writer. He wrote many letters, sermons, commentaries on scriptures, defences of christianity, his pamphlets on theology. Among his major works of interest for students of political theory or thought are the confessions and the city of God. The city of God is his greatest book. He completed this book in thirteen years. It was published in parts year by year. The confessions was a sort of spiritual autobiography written between 397 and 401, and is in the form of a prayer addressed to God. He thanks him for showing his light and laments the sins and follies that disfigured his life. The first to 10 chapters gives the details of his life and in the last 3, he details the story of creation, but the whole book is in praise of god. In the first 10 books he upholds the thesis that the God's are of no avail her or hereafter, in the last 12 chapters he develops the concept that everyman owes allegiance to one or the other of two cities—1. The city of this world, 2. The city of God, and then describes the origin, progress, destiny of those cities. In doing so, he explained the whole spiritual experience of mankind.

**3. St. Augustine's Aim or Purpose in Writing the City of God**

St. Augustine wrote the city of God to defend the Christian religion. He answered those who held Christianity was not at all responsible for Rome's fall. He expressed his opinion that Christianity was not at all responsible for Rome's fall. Nor was Rome's greatness due to her gods. It was the will of providence to make Rome great. God had made Rome great because he wanted to reward the Romans for their virtues. The pagan God's had not the power to defend Rome.[4]

According to Augustine, the downfall of Rome was not due to Cristianity. In his opinion, all earthly kingdoms pass away. St. Augustine wrote at very critical times in the history of Cristianity. He preached that the world could be saved from destruction by Christianity alone. According to St. Augustine the course of history had been determined by the will of God. St. Augustine preached that there was going on a struggle between light and darkness. This struggle was endless or ceaseless. According to St. Augustine the city of god alone is permanent kingdom, and earthly powers are temporary and transient and pass away.

**Influences on St. Augustine**

All the ideas of St. Augustine's political philosophy are not original. His political philosophy is influenced by that of other great writers. St. Augustine is a very impressive writer. He has shown remarkable success in changing the ideas of other philosophers to suit his philosophy.

We may note the following influences on St. Augustine :

**1. Influence of Plato**

From the great Greek philosopher Plato, the writer of the greatest treatise on political philosophy the republic, St. Augustine learnt the ideas of justice and the ideal state. According to Plato, Justice consists in the proper performance of functions by members of all the classes in the ideal state. There is justice when the workers work honestly, soldiers fight bravely and the philosophers rule wisely.[5]

St. Augustine applies this idea of justice to his philosophy. For him, justice has wider connotation. According to St. Augustine, Justice consists in conformity to a universal order. To conform to universal order is to obey the will of God. St. Augustine was influenced by Plato's idea of the ideal state and portrayed the city of god in his own words and style with a religious and spiritual colouring.

**2. St. Augustine was Influenced by Cicero's Ideas**

Cicero, the great Roman Orator and Lawyer, also influenced St. Augustine's thought. Cicero had preached that all men are members of one commonwealth—the commonwealth of the world, because all are bound by the common bond of reason. St. Augustine also preaches that all men belong to one commonwealth—the city of god. All men are united by love of God.[6]

**3. St. Augustine was also Influenced by Stoic Philosophy**

From the stoics, St. Augustine learnt the idea that man is a member of the state to which he belongs and also a member of human society to which all human beings belong. The individual should do his duty to both. The stoic philosophy of universal brotherhood, equality, sympathy and gentleness influenced St. Augustine's thought.

**4. The Teachings of Christianity**

St. Augustine adopted the Christian faith when he was 33. He was made the Bishop of Hippo. The doctrine of Christianity moulded his political ideas. He learnt from the Christian faith that human nature has two sides—the spiritual and secular side. To develop the spiritual side of human nature, there is the Church and for the development of the secular side of human nature, there is the state.

**The Philosophy of St. Augustine**

There are three principal ideas which can broadly summaries St. Augustines—Cosmology, Epistemology and Ethics. He was not primarily a political leader, he was not only a mystic, possessed a longing for the infinite, but also an ecclesiastical statesman.

The first of his central idea is the creation for from being motiveless or purposeless creation, therefore is God's act of love. All things that exist are therefore good. They reflect God being in varying degrees and therefore, they have varying degrees of goodness. Even matter, therefore, is essentially good for God made it evil does not lie in matter or in material existence. This we can see if we look inward and hear the inward of god. The Magister interior those will enable us to see the truth.

The second central idea of Augustine is that the source of knowledge does not lie outside, but it is inward. In this he followed Plato squarely. One we hear the word of God, we will be able to regulate our life accordingly and achieve the state of felicity or happiness or well being which is the universal desire for humanity.[7]

The third basic idea of Augustine is his ethical doctrine according to which we must subordinate what is lower to what is higher. The degrees are of being vary. (The principle enunciated above). These varying degrees of being lead to varying of goodness or value. The way to achieve the highest degree of goodness is to subordinate the lesser good to the higher or greater good, the lower to the higher, body to the spirit and spirit to god. Everything which exist is essentially good but relatively the thing the value it has. Since god created the universe for man's redemption it was his act of love. Love therefore, is the nature of man. It is the dynamic force which impels us to action. If it is properly directed it will never flow towards the lower or the flesh. Since everything is essentially good, everything can be used in the service of the Supreme God. All lesser goods are, therefore, to be used as means or aids towards the higher and higher, towards the highest which alone can really be enjoyed, for that is the 'end' of the scale. And because of the Supreme good is also the universal good, that is, the good of all, it can never be attained if we only seek or work for a private good of our own. Selfish pursuit of happiness, therefore, defeats its own end.[8]

The Supreme good St. Augustine says is God, man's perfection I love. God is love infinite 'a gape,' love tends to give, not take. Love therefore, is charity with humility. We should therefore, love each other as God loves us and this we can do if we derive the power of love from him, and not from lesser goods. There are two cities—earthly city, heavily city. Earthly by love of self, contempt of god, the heavenly by love of god. The earthly city glorifies itself, the heavenly in the lord. One seeks glory from man, but the greatest glory of the other is god, the witness of conscience. The one lifts up its head on its own glory, the other says to its God.[9]

## IMPORTANT, VITAL, SIGNIFICANT AND LASTING POLITICAL IDEAS OF ST. AUGUSTINE

### Introduction

We get a vivid and impressive picture of St. Augustine's

political ideas in the greatest of his books, the city of god. The great philosopher completed his great book in 13 years. He wrote this book to impress upon the minds of the people his firm conviction that the human race could be saved from destruction by Christianity alone. He also answered those people who thought that Christianity was the cause of fall of Rome. In a remarkable and forceful style, he defended Christianity and criticised the pagan Gods.

A brief account of St. Augustine's political ideas in given below :

**1. The City of God**

**(I) The Earthly and Heavenly Kingdoms**

St. Augustine gives a very clear picture of the city of god. According to St. Augustine, human nature has two side—the physical or bodily or secular and the spiritual side. Corresponding to the bodily side of human nature, there is earthly kingdom. In the earthly kingdom, our appetites are satisfied. All our possessive impulses find satisfaction in the earthly kingdom. The earthly kingdom is the society of human beings whose only interest is the satisfaction of the lower part of their nature. On the other side, there is city of God, corresponding to the spiritual side of human nature. In the city of God, there is heavenly peace and spiritual salvation. The city of God is not only heaven which is the goal of the Christians as their eternal home. According to St. Augustine, there is a counterpart of heaven here on this earth. This is the Church. The Church of the Christians is the city of God. According to St. Augustine the city of God is the kingdom of Christ and the earthy city is the kingdom of Satan. To him, the city of God will pass into eternal bliss, and the earthly city will be committed to eternal punishment.[10]

**(II) St. Augustine's View is Similar to and also Different from the Stoic View**

St. Augustine's doctrine of the city of God has a resemblance to the Stoic view expressed by the Roman philosopher Cicero that all men belong to the universe because they are bound by the common bond of being human beings. The eternal society of men transcends all limits of state, race or class.

According to Cicero, all men are members of this eternal and universal human society. According to St. Augustine, Gods plan was to make all men members of this society when he created the human race. But since the fall of man, only those who have received the grace of God can become members of the kingdom.

### 2. St. Augustine's Philosophy of History

St. Augustine is also famous and popular for his philosophy of history. He gives his philosophy of history in the first ten books of the city of God. A brief analysis of St. Augustine's philosophy of history is given below :

#### (I) There is a Divine will Behind All Events

According to St. Augustine, human history unfolds the will of God. St. Augustine thought that all events in the universe are caused and controlled by a divine will. God who is the creator of the universe determines forces and events of history. St. Augustine preached that nothing happens without God's will. The course of historical events is determined not by chance, but in accordance with the eternal purpose of the creator. St. Augustine believed that it was the will of god to establish the kingdom of god on earth. The history of the Church is march of God in the world.[11]

#### (II) All Events are Predestined, Predetermined and Preordained

According to St. Augustine, the events and happenings in the universe are predestined, predetermined and preordained. All events move in accordance with the preplanned plan of the creator of the universe.[12]

#### (III) Individual, A free Agent

Though St. Augustine believed in predestination and predetermination of events, at the same time, he thought that man is a free agent and is responsible for his evil actions.

### (IV) Struggle Between Good and Evil—Light and Darkness

According to St. Augustine, there is going on in this universe, a ceaseless struggle between good and evil—light and darkness. The secular empires of this world represent the forces of evil or darkness. These empires according to St. Augustine are temporary and transitory. They will pass away. The kingdom of God represents the forces of good or light. The secular empires of this world will perish, but the kingdom of God will last for ever.[13]

### (V) Christianity was not the Cause of Fall of Rome

In his book, the city of God, St. Augustine defended Christianity with forceful pen. He answered all those critics who said that Christianity was the cause of fall of Rome. According to St. Augustine, Christianity was not the cause of fall of Rome. The fall of Rome was the result of the will of God. St. Augustine was a great critic of paganism and the pagan gods. He expressed his opinion that the pagan God's had not made Rome great. They did not possess the power to save the Rome. Fall of Rome was in accordance with the divine will.[14]

## 3. St. Augustine's Views on the State

St. Augustine's views about the state are different from those of the Greek writers. He does not accept the view of the Greek philosophers that the basis of the state is justice.

A brief description of Augustine's ideas about the state is given below :

### (I) The State is a Remedy for Human Sin and Evil

According to Augustine, the divine will created the state as a remedy for evil and sin. The state exists to punish the evil-doers. Though the creator of the universe created the state to remedy sin, as an institution it did not represent sin.

### (II) Divine Origin of the State

St. Augustine is the supporter of divine origin of the state. The ruler deserves to be obeyed because he has a divine sanction.

At the same time, St. Augustine believes that the earthly states have degenerated into the kingdoms of Satan.

### (III) No Justice in a Non-Christian State, Justice Possible Only in a Christian State

According to St. Augustine, there can be no justice in a non-Christian state. The earthly state is inferior to the eternal state of the spirit.

### (IV) Obedience to the State is Necessary, So Long as the Orders of the Ruler do not come in Conflict with the Laws of Religion and Morality

St. Augustine does not accept the view that the state is an unnecessary evil. The state is necessary to protect property. The state gives rights and has the right to take back these rights. The state has a right to be obeyed. In case the decrees of the state violate laws of religion and morality, these laws of the state must be disobeyed. St. Augustine is of opinion that it is the duty of the individual to obey the state, but he has a more important duty to obey the Church which represents the will of God.[15]

### (V) Relation Between the State and the Church

Though St. Augustine expresses his opinion that the law of the Church is superior to that of the state, yet it he does not suggest subordination of the state to the Church. A Christian king stand in need of spiritual guidance from the Church. The state is essential for the Church because it creates favourable conditions for the functioning of the Church by promoting law and order.

## 4. St. Augustine's Views on Justice

St. Augustine elaborates his views on justice in his great book, the city of God.

A brief account of his views about justice is as follows :

### (I) Justice is Conformity to Order

According to St. Augustine, justice is conformity to order. He explains the meaning of justice by giving examples of the family, the state and the widest universal order.[16]

### (II) Justice in the Family

The family is the smallest and the first society to which the individual belongs. The family imposes an order upon its members. The indvduals who conform to that order are just. In other words, justice in the family consists in the obedience of its rules and performance of duties by all its members.[17]

### (III) Justice in the State

The state is of more universal order than the family. If the family revolts against the state, it is unjust. There will be justice in the state, when all its members conform to its laws. But that will be absolute justice.

### (IV) Absolute Justice in the Widest Order—Society of All Men in the Kingship of God

There is a wider society than the state. This is the widest order. This is the universal order. A state may be a strong state. Its members may obey its laws willingly. But there cannot be absolute justice even then. Absolute justice will prevail when the state conforms to the universal order. To conform to the universal order is to obey the will of God. Justice in the family and the state is only relative justice. Absolute justice consists in conformity to universal order.

### (VI) No Justice in Earthly Kingdoms and Pagan States

According to St. Augustine, true justice and peace can exist only in the city of God. There can be no justice in pagan states. Justice can prevail only in the Christian states.[18]

### (VII) St. Augustine Gives a Wider Meaning to Justice than Plato

While comparing Plato's and St. Augustine's conception of justice, Foster says that Augustine gives a wider meaning to justice than Plato. St. Augustine does not confine justice within the limits of the state, but thinks that justice is conformity to universal order. Justice for St. Augustine has an international connotation.[19]

## 5. St. Augustine's Views About Peace

St. Augustine has given a clear picture of his views about peace. A brief analysis of his views about peace is given below :

### (I) For Augustine, Peace has a Positive Meaning not a Negative One

We generally interpret peace in a negative way. We think that peace is the absence of war. To us, peace does not suggest any positive relation. We think that absence of hostile relations is peace. According to Augustine, peace is positive relation of love embracing all human beings concord. Just as, there cannot be war without enemies, similarly, there cannot be peace without partners.

### (II) Peace is the End of All Living Creatures

According to St. Augustine, all living creatures-men and beasts desire peace. St. Augustine is of opinion that all men seek peace by war. He thinks that the every wild beasts preserve peace with others in their kind.

### (III) Universal Peace

According to St. Augustine, the pagan states cannot realize universal peace. The peace which the state gives in only relative. It is only a means, not an end. Peace of the state creates conditions for love and service of God. The peace of the state is purely temporary. There is no permanent tranquility in the peace provided by the state. According to St. Augustine, there is a possibility of realizing universal peace if all human beings conform to the universal order and act in accordance with common love of God. Universal peace is the end of all living creatures. Universal peace cannot be brought about by common love of God. It is not possible to achieve universal peace by legal relations.[20]

### (IV) Peace of the Soul

According to St. Augustine, the end of the universe is peace, harmony and order. This is the highest end for all living creatures. But peace of life immortal is for superior to the peace of this world. The peace of the soul is far higher, nobler and better than the peace of the body. The superiority of the soul to the body is proved by the fact that God has given to man the right to rule over things without soul.[21]

### 6. St. Augustine's Views on Slavery

St. Augustine did not condemn slavery. He thought that slavery was the result of sin. St. Augustine did not regard slavery as a natural institution. God intended all men to be equal. But the fall of Adam deprived men of the right of equality. St. Augustine thought that the slave should not run away from his master. The slave should submit himself to the rule of the master. The slave should serve his master willingly, cheerfully and faithfully. According to St. Augustine, the institution of slavery is a collective retribution on the human race for the fall of humanity in Adamn. St. Augustine could not give a satisfactory justification for slavery. Therefore, his successors came to the conclusion that slavery could not be justified at all.[22]

### 7. St. Augustine's Views on Property

St. Augustine justified the institution of property. He did not regard property as a natural institution. According to him, property is a conventional institution. St. Augustine says that the individual should have as much property as is necessary of his essential needs. The possession of property was essential because it enabled the individual to perform his duties satisfactorily.

### Influence of St. Augustine

It has been said St. Augustine was the pioneer of political thinkers of the middle ages. His philosophy exercises a great influence on the political thought of the political philosophers of the middle ages. Next to St. Paul, St. Augustine is the most influencial Christian writer. His great book 'City of God' created unforgettable impressions on the minds of the people. This great book is the mine in which later writers have dug.

St. Augustine's most valuable contributions to political thought are given below :

### 1. St. Augustine was the First Great Political Philosopher to Discuss the Relation Between the Church and the State

St. Augustine was the first great political philosopher to discuss the relation between the Church and the state. He is the father of the Christian Commonwealth—The Holy Roman Empire. Throughout the middle ages, the most important question was that of the relation between the Church and the state.

### 2. St. Augustine gave the Idea that the Authority of the State was not Absolute

St. Augustine introduced a very important idea in the history of political thought. The authority of the state was not absolute. There was a higher authority than the state. This was the universal order. The laws of the state were binding on the individual and the individual was duty bound to obey them so long as these laws were in conformity with the universal order, otherwise, the individual had a right to disobey them.[23]

### 3. St. Augustine was the Pioneer of the Idea of Universalism

St. Augustine was the pioneer of the idea of universalism. He preached that there was a universal human society and the barriers of state, language, race etc. could not stand in the way of wider human society. The common bond among the members of universal human society was the love of God.

### 4. St. Augustine Established the Idea of the Superiority of the Church

St. Augustine established the idea of the superiority of the Church. According to St. Augustine, there is the city of god in heaven. But there is a counterpart of that heavenly city of God on earth. This counterpart is the Church. The Church gives peace of the soul. It gives salvation. It unfolds the nature of God in the world.[24]

### Conclusion

St. Augustine moulded the thoughts of many medieval rulers and political thinkers. He was the most important Christian thinker of his times.

## REFERENCES

1. According to St. Augustine, Life is a 'admixture' of joys and sorrows.
2. M.G. Gupta, History of Political Thought, pp. 40-45.
3. St. Augustine was a very wonderful, impressive, and powerful writer.
4. L.D. Abrol, Western History of Political Thought, p. 50-55.
5. Quoted by Sabine, A History of Political Theory, p. 79.
6. Duning, A History of Political Theories, p. 49.
7. Dunning, *op. cit.,* p. 57.
8. Greek Political Theory, p. 407.
9. According to St. Augustine, the earthly city lives 'after the flesh', it is formed by the love of self. The city of god lives after the spirit. Its members are humble lovers of god.
10. The earthly city is full of sorrows, and miseries.
11. St. Augustine said, Church is the march of God on the earth.
12. All events took place in this world according to the pre-plan of the god.
13. Augustine said joys and sorrows are just like the two parts of the same coin.
14. Christianity impressed upon the minds of the people that they had a spiritual as well as a temporal side of their life. It was the function of the state to take steps for the development of the temporal side of the life of the individuals. The responsibility of the Church was to take care of the spiritual side of the life of the individuals.
15. Dunning, A History of Political Theories, p. 158.
16. According to St. Augustine, the state is a remedy for human evil.
17. Absolute justice is conformity to universal order.
18. Peace of the soul is far superior to the peace of this world.
19. St. Augustine's great book 'City of God' created deep impressions on the minds of the people.

20. St. Augustine was the first great thinker to discuss the relation between the church and the state.
21. St. Augustine, City of God, *op. cit.,* pp. 66-68.
22. St. Augustine, *op. cit.,* p. 70-80.
23. Sabine, A History of Political Thought, pp. 93-94.
24. Gettel, A History of Political Theories, pp. 96-98.

# 6

# St. Thomas Aquinas

## (1225 A.D.—1274 A.D.)

### His Life

St. Thomas Aquinas who represents the totality of medieval thought was born at Roccasecca in the province of Nepals in 1225 A.D. and died in 1274 A.D. He was very intelligent and was gifted with sharp memory. The ambition of his parents was that he should have a bright career in the state. He belonged to a Lombard Norman family which was one of the most influencial in Southern Italy. His brothers held high ranks in the imperial army and most of his sisters had been married in illustrious families. He first studied in the Abbey School, and then he went as an Arts student of the University of Naples where he worked under Peter, the Irishman and Martin of Denmark. A few years later, he went to Cologne and Paris to continue his philosophical studies under Albert Magnus. In a large public debate his argumentation was so dramatic, persuasive and logical.[1]

In 1248 he became lecturer under the guidance of his teacher (Albert Magnus) and in 1249-50, he composed his first treatise on the principles of nature and on being and essence. In 1252, he became a graduate of Arts at the university of Paris and was appointed as a lecturer in Theology at the college of Jacobins at Paris. In 1256 he was appointed professor in theology at the Paris University and delivered numerous sermons in the various Churches of the French capital. Next year he got his doctorate *i.e.* Ph.D. in Theology. Meanwhile his reputation spread far and wide and his fame attracted disciplines from all parts of Europe. In 1259, he was appointed theological adviser and the lecturer to the Papal Court and King Louis IX and even invited him to take part in the private deliberations of his councils. He also studied Theology in Rome in a wider perspective. Along with this he continued to teach Theology in Paris, Bologna, Rome and Neples. In 1272, he was appointed director of the Naples Stadium. He died on March 7, 1274 at the age of 49 at Lyons. His doctrine was officially endorsed by the Papal encyclical of 1879 that of 1923. A controversial figure throughout his life-time, his writings are characterized by intellectual sharpness, powerful, dialectic, spirited style. The major portion of his remaining life was spent in Paris. He spent a part of his life in Italy also. He spent his life in "Study, Writing, Lecturing and Disputing".

**Works of St. Thomas Aquinas**

St. Thomas Aquinas was a voluminous writer. Though he died at a young age of 49, yet he wrote many excellent books. His famous books are the following :

**1. Summa Theologica**

This book is the greatest philosophical of St. Thomas Aquinas. In this great book St. Thomas Aquinas gives the juristic and ethical bases of politics. He has developed the ethical and juristic concepts very skillfully. These concepts are the starting points of his political philosophy. This is the most important of his works which are of interest in a study of political thought. Summa theological which contains his doctrines of law and the rule of princes which is purely political treatise. His theological deals with God and man in the form of man (Christ). It was his masterpiece which served as the last word on political, social, and ethical questions and as the supreme guide for the theologians and philosophers for centuries.

The Summa theological is divided into 3 parts : 1. The natural, 2. The moral and the 3. Sacramental. Part first deals with the nature, part second divided into two sub-parts—First section deals men from the earthly side as moral responsible agents possessing passions, sentiments and mental faculties. The second section deals with the seven virtues—1. Faith, 2.

Hope, 3. Charity, 4. Prudence, 5. Justice, 6. Fortitude, 7. Temperence.

Thus part IInd deals with general with general morality and the nature of men (based on Aristotles ethics) and goes on to the special moral problems those of theological or Christian nature. He also discusses at length the help by which God directs men to his immortal destiny. Following St. Augustine, he contends that Gods nature and not man's will is the source of good. Part III is in complete. It is a plan of sacraments and then he entered into the IVth sacrament when his death ended his career in 1274.

**2. Commentaries on the Politics of Aristotle**

In this book, St. Thomas Aquinas gives an exposition and interpretation of Aristotle's political philosophy and comments upon it.

**3. De-Regimine Principum or the Rule of Princes**

This is an unfinished book. St. Augustine died before completing this book. In this unfinished, St. Thomas Aquinas has presented a systematic study of political science.

**4. Summa Contra Gentiles**

In this book, St. Thomas Aquinas discusses classifications of laws, nature and purpose of the state and the relation between the Church and the state.

**His Method**

He was an empiricist. He adopt scientific method. Throughout his writings, he follows the method of argumentation.

## POLITICAL PHILOSOPHY OF ST. THOMAS AQUINAS

**Introduction**

**1. Greatest and the Ablest Writer of the 13th Century**

St. Thomas Aquinas was the greatest and the ablest writer of the 13th century. He wrote many books of which Summa Theologica and De Regimine principum are the most famous.

### 2. Combined Reason and Revelation

St. Thomas Aquinas combined reason and revelation in his philosophy. He brought about a reconciliation between the doctrines of the Church and the rational pagan philosophy. In his philosophy, we find a synthesis of revealed knowledge and rational principles.

### 3. Made Politics a Science and Modified Cicero's and Aristotle's Political Thought

In St. Thomas Aquinas hands, politics became a science with a true medieval method. He modified the politics of Aristotle and Cicero in the light of the Bible.

### 4. Greatest the Scholastics

St. Thomas Aquinas was the greatest of all scholastics. The scholastics combined the study of speculative philosophy and theology.

### 5. Presents a Reconciliation Between St. Augustine and Aristotle

According to Dunning, St. Thomas Aquinas presents a reconciliation between St. Augustine and Aristotle. St. Thomas Aquinas was a great disciple of Aristotle. On the principles of Aristotle's philosophy, he built the edifice of theological principles. He subordinated the secular state to the Church.

### 6. Systematic Philosopher-Brought About a Synthesis Between Different Philosophies

Foster says—Aquinas is one of the great systematic philosophers of the world. His was a work of synthesis, of putting together what had previously been apart, of imposing an architectonic design upon what had previously been more or less fragmentary.

## INFLUENCES ON AQUINAS

One of the greatest influences which moulded St. Thomas Aquinas political philosophy was Aristotle's philosophy. Besides Aristotle many other philosophers moulded his thought. The greatest influence on St. Thomas was that of the Bible. We can trace the influence of the Bible in all the writings of St. Thomas Aquinas. It is important to mention some of the philosophers who influenced the idea of St. Thomas Aquinas.

**1. The Stoics, Cicero and other Roman Lawyers**

The Stoics moulded his ideas about law. From the Roman philosopher, Cicero, he learnt a lot about natural law. Similarly, other Roman lawyers influenced his views.

**2. Influence of St. Augustine and Other Church Fathers**

The theological doctrines and philosophical ideas of St. Thomas Aquinas were influenced by the philosophy of St. Augustine, the great Christian thinker who wrote the city of God to defend Christianity. St. Thomas Aquinas is indebted to St. Augustine and other Church fathers for the idea that the state is subordinate to the Church.

**3. Influence of John of Salisbury**

St. Thomas Aquinas was influenced by the ideas of John of Salisbury who is famous for the view that the kings are bound by the law.

**4. Influence of His Teacher—Albert the Great**

St. Thomas Aquinas was greatly influenced by the ideas of his great teacher, Albert the Great. Under the influence of his teacher, he became a scholastic and learnt how to bring about a synthesis in different branches of knowledge—Ethics, Economics, Politics, Theology and Science. St. Thomas Aquinas combined faith with reason. He combined pagan doctrines with Christian philosophy.

**5. Influence of Aristotle**

St. Thomas Aquinas was a great disciple of Aristotle. He revived Aristotle's philosophy which had been forgotten for about a thousand years. He accepted many principles of Aristotelian philosophy and gave them a new shape in the light of the teachings of Christianity.

The following is a brief account of some of the principles of Aristotle's philosophy which St. Aquinas borrowed and modified in the light of Christian philosophy.

**1. Man is a Social Animal and the State is a Natural Institution**

Aristotle is famous for the dictum, man is a social animal. The man who can live alone is either a beast or a God. St. Thomas accepts Aristotle's dictum that man is a social animal and it is essential for him to live in society. Therefore, government is necessary because of social nature of man like Aristotle, St. Thomas Aquinas is also of opinion that the state is a natural institution. St. Thomas Aquinas does not accept the doctrine that the state is the result of fall of man. He rejects the idea that the state originated as a result of man's sin. He believed like Aristotle, that the state has evolved gradually. He adds to Aristotle's theory of Christian idea that the state was created by God. He believes in the evolutionary theory of Aristotle about the origin of the state but he also believes that the state was the creation of the Divine will. He is of opinion that "the power of the ruler is derived from God."

**2. There is End or Purpose in Man's Life and in the Universe**

Like Aristotle, St. Aquinas also believes that there is end or purpose in the universe. All things in nature are moving towards that end or goal or purpose. Human beings are also trying to attain their goal. The true character of human beings is realized when they reach their goal. Aristotle believes that reason is the highest faculty in man and enables him to realize his goal. Man is a rational animal. Rational contemplation is the goal of his life. St. Thomas Aquinas is of opinion that the highest faculty in man is not reason, but soul. The salvation of soul is the goal of human life. Reason cannot help man to attain salvation of soul. Only faith and grace of God can help man to realize salvation of soul. St. Thomas Aquinas's firm conviction is that salvation of soul is impossible unless faith and grace of God help reason.[2]

### 3. The State Exists to Make Good Life Possible for the Individuals

Aristotle believes that the state exists to promote conditions of good life for man. The state plays the most important role in the life of man. It makes him moral. Like Plato, Aristotle believes that the primary function of the state is to educate the citizens. St. Thomas Aquinas also believes that educating the people is a very important function of the state. St. Thomas Aquinas is a critic of the idea of the Church fathers that the function of the state is only negative. The function of the state, according to the Church fathers was to protect order, security and peace. St. Aquinas believes like Aristotle that the function of the state is positive. The state exists not only to make life possible, but also to make good life possible. The function of the state is to promote happiness of the individuals and to promote their moral development by educating them.

### 4. St. Thomas Aquinas Believes that the Church is More Important than the State

Though St. Thomas Aquinas agrees with Aristotle that the function of the state is positive—to promote happiness and good life of the individuals, yet he does not accept Aristotle's ideas that the state is the highest association and the only one to promote the good life of the individual. St. Thomas Aquinas rejects Aristotle's idea that the state embraces all the aspects of the life of the individual.

St. Thomas Aquinas points out that besides the state, there is Church to promote the welfare of the individuals. The Church is superior to the state. St. Thomas Aquinas assigns a higher place to the Church because the function of the Church is to promote the spiritual welfare of the people. According to St. Thomas Aquinas, the Church is the highest human institution. It is not the rival of the state, but is essential for its completion and perfection.

### 5. St. Thomas Aquinas is Influenced by Aristotle's Ideas About Justice

Both Plato and Aristotle are famous for their views on justice.

According to Plato, Justice prevails in the ideal state when the philosophers rule wisely, the soldiers fight bravely and the workers work honestly. Aristotle believes that justice is virtue in action. He gives two kinds of justice—complete justice and distributive justice. Complete justice is identical with the whole of moral life. Distributive justice means giving state offices and other good things of life according to the worth or merit of the individuals. Aristotle also talks of corrective justice which means giving to the individual what he has lost as a result of encroachment upon his rights by others. According to Aristotle, law is the expression of pure and passionless reason. The citizens should obey the laws of the state. St. Thomas Aquinas, like Aristotle, makes a distinction between distributive and corrective justice. St. Thomas Aquinas thinks that the laws of the state are the source of rights and justice. He makes natural laws superior to human laws. He is of opinion that in case human laws are not in conformity with the eternal, natural and divine laws, they are not valid.

## St. Thomas Aquinas—A Representative of the Middle Ages

St. Thomas Aquinas has been called a representative of the middle ages or the medieval period. In his philosophy, we can trace all the doctrines of the middle ages. He was the greatest of all the medieval thinkers.

### 1. The Famous Writers of the Middle Ages

The famous writers of the middle ages were Gregory VII, St. Bernard, and John of Salisbury. Gregory VII and John of Salisbury were the extremists. They stood for supremacy of the Church. They were popalists of the extremist type. To Gregory VII, justice meant unquestioned authority of Pope over the Church. He was of opinion that the humblest of the priests of Christ occupied a more exalted position than the greatest of secular rulers. According to John of Salisbury, the king drew his powers from the Church, because the kings authority came from God. He was in favour of a general control by the Pope over secular authorities but he was against any active interference of the Church in secular matters. St. Bernard also believed in the supremacy of the Church over the state. But he believed that the Pope should totally be interested in the spiritual matters and should not interfere in the work of the state.[3]

**2. St. Thomas Aquinas Also a Papalist**

St. Thomas Aquinas was also a papalist like writers of the middle ages. He was, however, not an extremist like Gregory VII and John of Salisbury. He was liberal in his views about the relations between the state and the Church. He was of opinion that the Church was superior to the state, but at the same time he preached that the Church should avoid interference in state matters unless there were very urgent and serious Causes for that interference.

**3. St. Thomas Aquinas was the Greatest of all Medieval Thinkers**

St. Thomas Aquinas was the greatest of all medieval thinkers. According to Foster, he was one of the great systematic philosophers of the world. He represents the totality of medieval thought.

We may trace the following medieval elements in the teachings of St. Thomas Aquinas :

**1. The Doctrine of Two Swords**

The Doctrine of the two swords was supported by the writers of the middle ages. According to this doctrine, it was necessary to separate spiritual and secular authorities. The Church satisfied the spiritual needs of man. The state satisfied the secular needs. It was a pagan practice to combine the spiritual and secular or temporal authorities. The state and the Church are separate organizations. In case of conflict, the Church should have superior authority. Thomas Aquinas believed like the supporters of the doctrine of two swords that the spiritual and secular authorities should be separated and the authority of the Church should prevail whenever there was a conflict between the Church and the state. Like all medieval thinkers, St. Thomas Aquinas supported papal authority.[4]

## 2. Supporter of Monarchy

Like other medieval thinkers, St. Thomas Aquinas believed that monarchy was the best form of government, because it was a stable form of government. St. Thomas Aquinas was not in favour of absolute monarchy. He thought of limitations on the authority of the monarch. The laws were the greatest limitation on the authority of the monarch. St. Thomas Aquinas thought that the monarch was bound by the Divine laws. The medieval thinkers exalted the institution of monarchy, not the personality of the monarch. The people had the right to criticize and disobey the unjust monarch. Like the medieval thinkers, St. Thomas Aquinas believed that it was the duty of the king to protect the people and to promote their happiness. Service of the people was regarded as the main duty of the king.

## 3. Universalism

The Medieval thinkers believed in the universal or cosmopolitan society. The Church represented the spiritual side of human life all over the world. The state was a representative of the secular side of life. The pope was the head of the Church and the emperor was the head of the state. Both the pope and the emperor were representatives of universal human society. St. Thomas Aquinas believed in one universal society. Thus, he represented medieval thinkers in this respect also.

## 4. St. Thomas Aquinas was the Greatest Scholastic

St. Thomas Aquinas was a great exponent of universalism. He was also the greatest representative of Aristotelianism. There was one more element in his teachings. He was the best representative of scholasticism. He was the greatest scholastic. In order to understand medieval thought it is essential to understand scholasticism. Scholasticism is the master key to the understanding of medievalism.

Scholasticism was a product of medieval universities in Europe.[5] The main contribution of scholasticism was synthesis of different branches of knowledge. Knowledge according to the scholastics was very comprehensive and covered within its scope various branches of knowledge. Knowledge included within its scope moral, social, economic, political and many other problems. As a scholastic philosopher, St. Thomas Aquinas brought about a synthesis between Aristotellian philosophy and Christian Theology.

The scholastic philosophers thought that knowledge was a building with three storeys. At the top-story of this building of knowledge was theology which controlled all other branches of knowledge. Sciences were at the ground of this building of knowledge and in the first floor was philosophy. In other words, in the system of knowledge theology occupied the first position, then came philosophy and last position was that of sciences. The function of philosophy was to bring about a correlation between the fundamental principles of sciences. Philosophy and Sciences are guided by reason. Theology which is guided by Divine reason must control and guide philosophy and sciences.

This idea can be explained by a simple diagram. Building of knowledge having three storeys :

1. Theology → Guided by Divine Reason
2. Philosophy → Guided by Reason
3. Sciences → Guided by Reason

St. Thomas Aquinas was a great representative of this philosophy. He tried to complete Aristotle's reason based philosophy by faith. He subordinated the state to the Church.

In all his teachings, we find a scholastic point of view. Like a true scholastic, he subordinated reason to faith. St. Thomas Aquinas has been called the father of scholasticism.

Sabine says, Thomas's philosophy expresses most maturely the convictions, moral and religious, upon which medieval civilization was founded.

## ST. THOMAS AQUINAS LEADING POLITICAL IDEAS

### Origin of Society and State

Theology is his life breath. He said there was God and that his existence could be proved without a reference to revelation. His arguments are all teleological. His argument of motion is that anything which is moved by some other thing movers and moved. There is a first source of movement which is moved by nothing else, *i.e.* God. Hence he conclude that there is the first and uncaused cause *i.e.* God. Then he deduces the existence of God from the theory of possible and necessary existence. Some existences are possible and not necessary, but they may exist or not exist, being generated and corrupted. There would be no ground for possible existence. There must, therefore, be something which is necessary *i.e.* God. Finally, there is the theory of degree of quality or value. Something's are more or less good more or less true and more or less excellent. Now more or less shows that there should be "most" and that "most" is the most true, good and excellent *i.e.* God.

St. Aquinas said, society is the efficient cause of the state or government. Rule is the law of nature. Everything is ruled by something, by something principle. In a man the body is ruled by mind or soul. Soul or mind is ruled by reason. Society must also be ruled.

### Origin, Nature and End of the State

St. Thomas Aquinas is very famous for his views about the origin and nature of the state. He bases his views on this subject on Aristotelian philosophy. At the same time, he shows an influence of the Christian Doctrines. Society is natural institution. State on the contrary is made by man so that his essential purpose of a higher life is realized. A govt. can go right or wrong. If the government is right and just, it is appropriate for freedom. If it is motivated by selfishness of the rulers, it is unjust and perverted. Thus, the end of the state is thus, the good of the governed and supreme good is happy life in heaven for which this life is a preparation. Happiness lies not only in virtue but also in the availability of adequate material goods—a sufficient supply of the necessaries of good living. The government should maintain peace and order without which virtue will not be possible ensuring good action and securing those external conditions without which good life is not possible.

St. Thomas Aquina's views about the origin and nature of the state are given below :

**1. The State is not the Result of Sin**

St. Thomas Aquinas does not accept the traditional Christian view that the state is the result of sin or fall of man. He rejects the idea that the state was created by God to punish men for their sins. The state, according to Thomas Aquinas is not an evil, but it is a positive good. St. Thomas Aquinas rejects the idea of Augustine and other Church fathers that there was no state in the state of innocence and the state was created by God because he wanted to punish men for sin and evil.

**2. The State is the Result of Social Instinct of Man**

The state is a natural institution. St. Thomas Aquinas is a disciple of Aristotle. He is Aristotle renamed. He is a Christianized Aristotle. We find influence of Aristotle's philosophy on St. Thomas views about the origin and nature of the state.

St. Thomas Aquinas follows Aristotle and declares that man is a social animal, and the state is a natural institution. Like Aristotle, he says that the rule of the superiors over the inferiors is natural. It is for the good of the inferiors that they should be ruled by superiors. For this reason, he agrees with Aristotle that educating the citizens is a very important function of the state. The state is natural because no man is self-sufficient. Man is in need of help of others for the satisfaction of his needs. The state is a system of mutual, exchange of services. It is founded for the sake of good life. Many callings make a contribution to this good life.

The central point in St. Thomas's argument about the origin and the nature of the state is that, the state not the result of sin of man, it came into existence for the fulfilment of human nature which is social.

### 3. St. Thomas Aquinas Also Believes in the Divine Origin of the State

Though St. Thomas Aquinas accepts Aristotle's view that the state is the result of social nature of man and is a natural institution, yet he shows influence of Christian doctrines and adds to the Aristotelian view the doctrine of the divine origin of the state. St. Thomas Aquinas believes that the state is created and established by God. It is the result of social instinct of man. God planted the social instinct in man. Therefore, God is the creator of the state. According to St. Thomas Aquinas, political authority is derived from God who is the creator, the Governor, the controller and the director of the universe. St. Thomas Aquinas is a firm believer in St. Paul's dictum, that "There is no power but of God."

### 4. St. Thomas Aquinas is not in Favour of a Small City-state

St. Thomas Aquinas is not in favour of a small city-state. He believes that a small city-state cannot make effective arrangements for defence. Therefore, St. Thomas Aquinas shows his preference for larger kingdoms.[6]

## FUNCTIONS AND CLASSIFICATIONS OF THE GOVERNMENT

The end of government determines its functions. The end is happiness. Happiness means virtue. One ruler may be lord but his successor may be bad. The rulers, therefore, should carefully ensure sound succession in various offices. The ruler must frame and enforce such laws as can stop wickedness and as may conduce virtue. The law abiding must be rewarded and the offenders must be punished. Good life must be impeded by external invasions, which can destroy the whole society. The government must keep the people safe from enemies and takes suitable steps for defence. For the good life of the individual two things are needed—1. Fundamental, *i.e.* virtue, 2. Instrumental and secondary is material goods. Poverty and exploitation may hinder the advancement of the community. He recommends a sound equitable theory of just wages and just prices.

Further, illiteracy is another serious impediment to good life. The rulers therefore, must, try to educate the people under their charge. Education leads to virtue. In this Aquinas followed Aristotle. In his tract De-Magistro, he spells out his theory of education. The function of a teacher is analogous to that of a physician. The physician is to heal the patient, and the teacher to learn his pupil. The pupil must be self-active in learning. Teaching can only assist this process, it cannot be a substitute for it.

Finally, Aquinas says to ruler whatever is wrong, to supply whatever is lacking to strive to perfect whatever can be improved.

## CLASSIFICATION OF GOVERNMENTS

He accepted traditional classification of governments monarchy and tyranny, Aristocracy and oligarchy, polity and democracy, but he has shown preference to monarchy as the best form of government. A king is the father of the people. Kingship is the best form of government not only because of scriptures but on rational grounds. It can establish unity which no other form of government can achieve. Numerous rulers will pull in various opposite directions and a happy life would be torn asunder. Again, all natural government is by one—the heart rules the body as the reason rules the soul. Society is derived from one God. Government is art and art is a reflection of nature which is ruled by one. But the king, says, Aquinas should be elected by the people and assisted by a nobility based on the possession of eminent virtue. He should be subject to (guiding force) of human law.

Sovereignty, so to say, is derived from one source *i.e.* God from the theological point of view. From one source people from the political point of view. It is best embodied in one principle *i.e.* Monarchy. Sovereignty is therefore, indivisible. That is one aspect.

Secondly, sovereignty is the source of positive law as we will shortly see. Aquinas said apart from the divine law, natural law, there is a positive law. This law must fulfill four requirements.

1. It must be derived from natural law, 2. It must be for the common good, 3. It must be framed and promulgated by the government and 4. It must serve as a directive for human acts of justice (while divine law and natural law regulate all human actions).

St. Thomas Aquinas starts with two bases for classifying the governments :

1. Slavery is the result of sin. Whether the supremacy of man over man was the result of his sin which resulted in his slavery. According to St. Thomas Aquinas, slavery is the result of sin of man and is a punishment to the human race. 2. The state is the result of social instinct. Whether the rule of man over man was the result of social instinct. According to St. Thomas Aquinas, the result of social instinct is civil government.

A brief account of St. Thomas classification of governments is given below :

1. Form of civil government. In his book De Regimine Principium (The rule of princes), he gives the following forms of civil government.

*(a)* Sacredotal and Royal

*(b)* Royal

*(c)* Political

*(d)* Economic

2. Examples and explanation of these forms of civil governments. Papacy is an example of the first form of civil government. The distinction between royal and political form is that between governments without law and governments subject to law. St. Thomas Aquinas does not explain the fourth form of civil governments.

3. St. Thomas Aquinas follows Aristotles classification of Governments :

Though St. Thomas's classification of governments is not clear, yet a very careful study of this subject reveals to us that he follows Aristotle's classification of governments. Like Aristotle, he believes that the governments can be classified into two kinds—those is which the rulers rule for the good of the people and those in which the rulers rule for their own good. In other words, like Aristotle, St. Thomas Aquinas classifies governments into good or normal and bad or perverted. Normal governments are classified into monarchy (Rule of one), Aristocracy (Rule of a few rich) and polity (Rule of many). Perverted governments are classified into tyranny, oligarchy and democracy. St. Thomas Aquinas is of opinion that monarchy is the best form of government. Tyranny according to him is the worst form of government.

Here we find a difference of opinion between St. Thomas Aquinas and Aristotle. According to Aristotle the best practicable state is polity (The rule of the middle class).

According to St. Thomas Aquinas, Monarchy is the best form of government. He gives the following reasons to support his view.

1. **The argument of unity.** St. Thomas Aquinas argues that the end of society is unity. Therefore, unity is the most essential principle in organization of the government. Unity is peace. The good of the society consists in unity. Only in monarchy, this unity can prevail. The monarch is a unit. He is the symbol of unity.

2. **Monarchy is a stable form of government.** St. Thomas Aquinas is of opinion that monarchy is the best form of government because it has the merits of stability and efficiency. There is a danger of anarchy, confusion and order in other forms of government, but there is no such danger in monarchy.

3. **Argument of one God.** St. Thomas Aquinas argues that just as one God rules over the entire universe, similarly one monarch should rule over the state.

**4. Argument of the Heart.** St. Thomas gives another argument on the basis of analogy. Just as the heart rules over the other parts of the body, similarly, the monarch should rule over his kingdom.

**5. Argument on the basis of experience.** According to St. Thomas Aquinas, monarchy is the best form of government because there is the advantage of continuity of experience. One monarch learns from the experience of the other and it becomes easy to take adequate steps for stability of government and for promoting the welfare of the people.

**6. According to St. Thomas Aquinas—the Ruler is not Absolute.** According to St. Thomas Aquinas, the ruler is not absolute. The ruler's authority is created by God and he owes his responsibility to him. St. Thomas Aquinas thinks that the ruler is responsible to God who is the author of all law on which the authority of the king rests. According to St. Thomas Aquinas, the Pope is the representative of God on earth and the ruler is subordinate to him. St. Thomas Aquinas limits the authority of the ruler in another way also. He says that the people have the right to remove the tyrant.

**7. St. Thomas's views on Tyranny.** According to St. Thomas Aquinas, the worst evil of monarchy is that it may become tyranny. St. Thomas Aquinas thinks that tyranny is the worst, form of government. He does not accept John of Salisbury's view that tyrants should be killed. In his opinion, killing tyrants will encourage bad men who kill even kings and will lead to anarchy. The tyrant should be removed peacefully by the combined efforts of all the people.

## FUNCTIONS OF THE GOVERNMENT

### Introduction

According to St. Thomas Aquinas, rulership is an office or a trust for the whole community. He is justified to continue as a ruler because as long as he performs the duties and functions which have been assigned to him by God from whom he has derived power.

Some of the important functions of the ruler, according to Thomas Aquinas, are the following :

**1. Promotion of Common Good**

It is the foremost duty of the ruler to promote common good. The ruler is duty-bound to subordinate his personal good to the common good. He has been given power and authority by God to make the people happy. He has been made head of the community by God Almighty, the creator of the universe so that he may dedicate himself to the service of the people and take all steps to add to their happiness and good.

**2. Promotion of Right Living**

The ruler has supreme control over secular matters. It is therefore, his duty to take adequate steps for establishing, maintaining and promoting right living among the people. It is the most important duty of the ruler to take care that virtuous and happy life is promoted among all sections of people. In other words, the ruler should undertake the function of educating the people. People should be taught morality and virtue. They should be trained to lead a virtuous life.

The ruler should never forget that it is his honest duty to remove all those hindrances and obstacles which block the path of good and moral life of the people. He should be fully aware of the wrongs, evils and abuses which hinder God life of the people.

**3. Promotion of Unity Which is called Peace**

A very urgent of the ruler is to make efforts to promote unity which is called peace. In no case should the ruler allow factions and dissensions in any shape. Political system can be excellently organized if there is unity an permanence. If the ruler allows factions and dissensions to take root in the state, there is the danger of anarchy. To save the state from anarchy, confusion and disorder. It is the duty of the ruler to crush all factions and dissensions. So that the unity of the state may be preserved. If the unity of the state is shaken, the ruler has no justification to continue as a ruler. The idea of the unity of the state was borrowed by St. Thomas Aquinas from the Greek philosophers.

### 4. To Maintain Law and Order in the State

Another very important of the ruler is to maintain law and order in the state and to make all arrangements for the protection of the life and property of the individuals. St. Thomas Aquinas suggests in Roman idea that the prince should keep the roads in his kingdom safe and free.

### 5. Defence of the Country

It is also the duty of the ruler to defend the dominion against external foes. The ruler should always be prepared to meet the threat to the safety of the state. He should take all precautions against foreign aggression.

### 6. To Provide Enough Food and Clothing to the People

It is the duty of the ruler to take care that the people are provided sufficient food and clothing and are properly clothed and fed.

### 7. The Prince should Introduce a System of Rewards and Punishments

It is the duty of the ruler to secure obedience from the people. One very effective way of securing obedience is to introduce a system of rewards and punishments. The ruler should reward the worthy and deserving people and should punish those who violate the laws. It is the duty of the ruler to see that all functions of administration and judicature are properly performed.

### 8. Introducing Coinage, Weights and Measures

A very important duty of the ruler is to introduce special coinage and to introduce weights and measures in his kingdom. St. Thomas suggests this function on grounds of expediency. He says that there will be less litigation if weights and measure sin the markets of the state are fixed by the government. Government weights and measures will lessen the chances of litigations and quarrels. St. Thomas also refers to the Bible to prove the necessity of weights and measures. "God had ordered all things by numbers, weights and measures."

**9. To Help the Poor and Needy**

It is the duty of the ruler to help the poor and the needy. He must give alms to the poor. St. Thomas argues that the princes owe a debt to people and God on account of the sins which they are likely to commit on account of possession of power and wealth. By giving charity they will discharge their debt.

**Conclusion**

St. Thomas Aquinas gives a long and elaborate list of the functions of the government. These are the positive functions of the government. Though he wrote about these functions many countries ago in different circumstances and on different grounds, yet the students of political science can read the lessons of the functions of a welfare state in the elaborate list of the functions of government mentioned and explained by the Christianized Aristotle, the Sainted Aristotle, the scholastic philosopher—St. Thomas Aquinas.

## RELATION BETWEEN THE CHURCH AND THE STATE

**Introduction**

The medieval age was a period of controversy between the Church and the state.[7] The Church represented the spiritual side of the life and the state represented the secular side of the life. The question under discussion was what should be the relation between these two organizations the spiritual power and the secular power. We may describe St. Thomas Aquinas's views under the following sub-headings :

**1. St. Thomas Aquinas—A Papalist, Advocated Supremacy of the Church**

St. Thomas Aquinas was a papalist. He subordinated the Church to the state. He thinks that the Church is final authority in matters of belief. Therefore, it should have superiority over the state. St. Thomas Aquinas says, "The state is not independent of the Church, but is subordinate to it in so far as their spheres overlap."

According to St. Thomas Aquinas, it is the duty of the political ruler to administer secular affairs in such a way so as to further God's will. He advocates that the officials of the state must follow the divine law of the Church. The officers of the state must be subordinate to the priests.

**2. Salvation not Possible Without Church**

According to St. Thomas Aquinas, the function of the government is to enable people to lead a virtuous life so that they may attain salvation. To attain salvation without the help of the Church is impossible even for the most virtuous man. Therefore, the Church is superior to the state.

**3. Thomas Aquinas's Arguments for Subordinating the State to the Church—The Example of the Carpenter and the Pilot**

St. Thomas Aquinas supports his idea of subordinating the state to the Church by saying that the state is like the carpenter and the Church is like the pilot of the ship. The ship is controlled and guided by the pilot. The carpenter has to obey the pilot. Both the carpenter and the pilot are necessary for taking the ship to its goal. Both the Church and the state are necessary for happiness and virtuous life of men. Just as the pilot is superior to the carpenter, similarly, the Church is superior to the state. The king should be controlled and guided by the Church. In other words, the king should obey the Pope.

**4. The Spirit Rules Over the Matter**

According to St. Thomas Aquinas, the spirit is superior to matter and rules over it. The spirit blessedness can be attained only through the Church of Christ. The Pope represents the spirit and is the head of the Church. The king represents the matter and is the head of the state. The Pope is superior to the king. The king should obey the Pope.

**5. The Pope had the Authority to Punish the King**

St. Thomas Aquinas thought that the Pope had full authority to punish the king if he did not obey him. A king who was disobedient to the pope could be excommunicated. The pope had the authority to tell the subjects not to obey the king who disobeyed his orders.

**6. The Pope had Territorial Sovereignty**

The Pope was the head of the Church. As head of the Church, it was his right to possess lands. He was not subordinate to the king even in his right of property. He was the sovereign over his lands. He was independent of the king.

**7. St. Thomas Aquinas—A Moderate Papalist**

Though St. Thomas Aquinas justified the superiority of the Church over the state and thought that the Pope had a right to guide and direct the king, yet he was a moderate papalist. He preached that the king was created by the will of God. He accepted the view that in secular matters, the king should enjoy a good deal of independence. According to St. Thomas Aquinas, there is no justification for disobedience of a pagan king by the Christian subjects.

## THEORY OF ST. THOMAS AQUINAS LAW

### Introduction

St. Thomas Aquinas's theory of law is a mixture of the ideas of Aristotle, the Stoics, Cicero, the Roman Imperial Jurists and St. Augustine. Like a true scholastic philosopher, St. Thomas Aquinas has combined the ideas of different philosophers. He has given exactness to those concepts and has overcome the vagueness which we may find in the writings of his predecessors on the subject of law.

St. Thomas Aquinas defines law as an ordinance of reason for the common good, promulgated by him who has the care of a community. MacIwain mentions the following elements in St. Thomas Aquinas's definition of law :

*(a)* Law is precept of practical reason.

*(b)* Law is promulgated by the ruler.

*(c)* The ruler rules over a perfect community.

*(d)* The perfection of the community is in the Aristotelian sense.

The community is more comprehensive than the household. St. Thomas Aquinas conception of law is broader than that of the medieval thinkers. He is of opinion that the law applies to the entire universe. The total universe is one rational unity and is governed by one law. The law which has different forms operates under the divine guidance. According to St. Thomas Aquinas, there is no opposition between human law and divine law. Human law is related to divine law. The basis of human law is human reason. The basis of divine law is divine reason or faith or revelation.[8]

There was absolutely no antithesis between reason and faith. There was ever-lasting unity between the two.

### Implications of His Theory of Law

St. Thomas Aquinas, the Sainted Aristotle, the Christianized Aristotle, the great doctor of the Church is at his best in enumerating the conditions or factors which are essential for the validity of the positive law. These are the implications of his theory of law.

1. **Law is related to reason.** St. Thomas Aquinas says that law is a rule and standard of human action. Therefore, law is essentially related to reason. Law is a command. Command comes from reason. Therefore, law is a thing of reason.

2. **The end of law is common good.** Law is the rule of human conduct. Ultimate end of human conduct is common happiness. Therefore, law must always be ordained for common good.

3. **Law can be created by the multitude or by the prince acting for the multitude.** St. Thomas Aquinas is of view that the law aims at the common good. Therefore, law can be created not by the reason of a single individual, but it can be created by a reason of a multitude. It can also be created by the reason of the prince who takes care of the interests of the multitude.

**4. Law should be brought to the notice of those who are subject to it.** St. Thomas Aquinas is of opinion that law should be promulgated and brought to the notice of those who are subject to it. In this way, law will have obligatory force. The essence of St. Thomas Aquinas's theory of law is that, its aim is common good and that it should be made and enforced by the multitude or by the ruler who takes care of the interests of the multitude and who acts on behalf of the multitude.

**Classification of Law**

According to St. Thomas Aquinas, law can be classified in the following way :

Sir, Thomas Aquinas classification of law can be explained with the help of the following table :

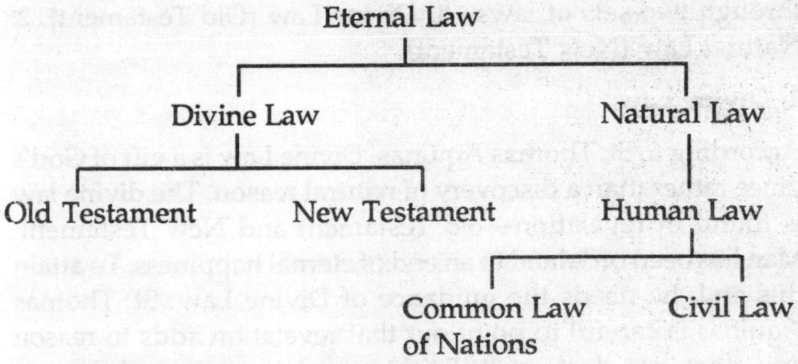


A brief account of the different types of law as explained by St. Thomas Aquinas is given below :

**1. Eternal Law**

At the top is the Eternal Law.

**(I) God Governs the Entire Universe Through Eternal Law**

St. Thomas Aquinas says that eternal law is identical with reason of God. He begins with eternal law which comes from divine reason and which is unknowable to us in its perfection as it is in God's mind. Eternal law is truth in itself. Animate kingdom is governed by eternal law. Inanimate kingdom is governed by eternal law. The entire universe is governed by

God through eternal law. St. Thomas Aquinas is of opinion that eternal law is cosmic. It regulates the earthly and heavenly spheres. It has different ways of functioning in the rational and irrational worlds.[9]

**(II) Eternal Plan of Divine Wisdom**

It is the eternal plan of divine wisdom by which the whole creation is ordered.

**(III) Human beings cannot know the Eternal Law Completely**

St. Thomas Aquinas is of opinion that human beings cannot know the eternal law in its perfection because it is in God's mind. We can know it part by part by revelation and by operation of our reason. Eternal law is expressed through divine law and natural law. The eternal law in other words, expresses through two sets of laws—1. Divine Law (Old Testament), 2. Natural Law (New Testament).

**2. Divine Law**

According to St. Thomas Aquinas, Divine Law is a gift of God's grace rather than a discovery of natural reason. The divine law is found in revelation—old Testament and New Testament. Man has been ordained to an end of eternal happiness. To attain this end, he needs the guidance of Divine Law. St. Thomas Aquinas is careful to point out that revelation adds to reason and does not destroy it. Faith completes reason. Whereas Natural Law is applicable to all human beings, Divine Law revealed by God only to his chosen people.[10]

**3. Natural Law**

According to St. Thomas Aquinas, Natural Law is a reflection of divine reason in creating things. Each man's heart has the dictates of natural law in it. This type of law helps us to know the distinction between good and evil. It also helps us to do good and to avoid evil. Man lives in society because natural law helps him to understand that man is a social animal. All beings are moved by this law and want to lead a good and perfect life according to their nature. Natural Law also means that man has a desire to lead a kind of life in which he may realize his rational nature. Natural Law gives the idea of self-preservation. It gives rise to the desire of getting children and nourishing them. It helps men to seek truth and develop their intelligence. Natural Law is nothing else than the participation of rational creatures in the eternal law.

Natural Law consists of principles of action, self-evident, infallible and unalterable. These principles have been promulgated by God. "God instilled these principles is man's mind so as to be known to him naturally." According to Thomas Aquinas, neither eternal law nor natural law is positive. Neither of these two laws was consciously adopted at a particular time or place. St. Thomas Aquinas is of opinion that neither eternal law nor natural law is obligatory in character.

In short, according to St. Thomas Aquinas, Natural Law consists of principles of action self-evident, in fallible, unalterable, promulgated by God. Natural Law comprises those precepts which mankind is able to formulate, namely, the preservation of one's own good, and pursuit of knowledge of God. It may be rested on purely rational and ethical foundations. Little theology is involved in it. It is unknown to vast numbers infact.

**4. Human Law**

According to St. Thomas Aquinas, human law is positive and a man-made law. It's source is Natural Law. Natural Law is superior to human law. Human Law is valid as long as it does not violate Natural Law. Human Law recognizes the fact that natural is planted in the hearts of all men. Human Law is applicable only to human beings.

It is the particular application of the Natural Law. It is enacted by will and rests for its basis on a social compact. One by very nature is Nature Law, the other, certain compact among men, and this is called positive law. The positive law comprises closely akin to Natural Law, derived from the Natural Law, involves local and temporal determinations and draws its force from human enactment *e.g.* that a given crime should be punished in a particular manner.

Then he proceeds to examine the conditions and factors which alone can qualify a positive law to be a valid law. He arrives at four conditions on which the validity of positive law depends.

1. It is necessarily related to reason,
2. Its ultimate end is the common good or happiness,
3. It must be created by reason,
4. It must be obligatory force, that it should be promulgated and brought to the notice of those who are subject to the law.

He said, Human Law is of two kinds :

1. Law of Nations,
2. Civil Law.

Attributes of Human Law. St. Thomas Aquinas mentions four attributes of human law :

(I) It is based on reason.

(II) It is ordained for common good.

(III) It is created by the reason of the multitude or by reason of the prince acting on behalf of the multitude.

(IV) It should be promulgated and brought to the notice of those who have to obey it. This will give obligatory force to the law.

St. Thomas Aquinas defines civil law as an ordinance of human reason for the common good, promulgated by one who has the care of the community. St. Thomas Aquinas gives to customs, the force of law. Custom according to him, is also the result of reason and has the power of abolishing or changing law.

According to St. Thomas Aquinas, there are two limitations on Civil Law :

The first limitation of Civil Law, according to St. Thomas Aquinas, is that it must always conform to Natural Law because Natural Law is higher than and superior to Civil Law.

Another limitation which St. Aquinas places on Civil Law is that he restricts its application only to the secular or temporal side of human life. The spiritual side of man's life does not come under the control of Civil Law. It is controlled by Divine Law.

## THEORY OF KNOWLEDGE

St. Thomas Aquinas was a rationalist through and through distinguished between faith and reason. Yet, he did not hold faith and reason are mutually antagonistic. Thomas placed the natural law is evident to reason, subordinate to it, but not in conflict with Eternal Law and Divine Law. There is no contradiction between faith and reason for the source of both is God. It is relative (fait) to man's present state. Reason gives full in sight. On this distinction between faith and reason is grounded the distinction between theology and science or Metaphysics. He established supremacy of reason. By uniting God, reason, nature and man, he set in motion what later on came to be called enlightenment. Aquinas cannot be held responsible by any stretch of reasoning or imagination.

## THEORY OF JUSTICE

St. Thomas Aquinas is famous for his views about justice. The following is a brief account of St. Thomas Aquinas's views about justice.

According to St. Thomas Aquinas justice is the basis of law. Law is the channel through which justice is expressed. He follows Aristotle and says that justice is "the fixed and perpetual will to give to every one his own right." Like Aristotle, St. Thomas Aquinas also believes that justice is proportionate equality. Like Aristotle, St. Thomas Aquinas draws a distinction between corrective and distribute justice. According to St. Thomas Aquinas, the laws have a great influence on justice. If the laws in a state are good, healthy and sound, justice will prevail in that state. On the other hand, if the laws are unhealthy and unsound, there will be no justice. Thus, there is a close relationship between justice and law.

## CONTRIBUTIONS OF ST. THOMAS AQUINAS TO POLITICAL THOUGHT

### Introduction

St. Thomas Aquinas was the greatest political thinker of his times. He was one of the greatest political thinkers of all times. He has been called the second Aristotle, the Christianized Aristotle, the Sainted Aristotle, Aristotle re-named.

A brief account of St. Thomas Aquinas's contributions to political thought is given below :

### 1. Revived Aristotle Philosophy, Represented Middle Ages, was a True Scholastic

To St. Thomas Aquinas goes the credit of reviving Aristotle's philosophy in Europe. This philosophy had been forgotten for about a thousand years. St. Thomas Aquinas brought it back to Europe. St. Thomas Aquinas was a representative of the middle ages. He was a scholastic philosopher and tried to bring about a synthesis between Aristotle's philosophy and Christian teachings, between faith and reason.

### 2. Some of his Immortal Ideas

St. Thomas Aquinas's theory of knowledge, his views about the functions of government, his classification of governments and above all, his classification of law and his views about justice have made him an immortal thinker in political science. He has adopted a middle position between the Greek view of Law as passionless reason and the view of the modern jurists about law as the command of the sovereign. St. Thomas Aquinas thinks that law is obeyed because its source is reason and it is enforced by the ruler. This idea about law is really a great contribution to political thought.

### 3. St. Thomas Aquinas is a Forerunner of Many Political Philosophers

St. Thomas Aquinas is a forerunner of many political philosophies. The student of political science can learn lessons of democracy and constitutional government in his political thought. When we read his description of the functions of the government, we feel that he is the forerunner of the modern concept of the welfare state. St. Thomas was an individualist also. He gave due importance to the individuals happiness and pointed out that the aim of life was the attainment of salvation for the soul.

### 4. St. Thomas Tried to Bring A Reconciliation Between the Church and the State

One of the greatest contributions of St. Thomas Aquinas was that he tried to bring about a reconciliation between the Church and the state. St. Thomas Aquinas was a papalist. He subordinated the Church to the State. He advocated that the king should obey the pope and should administer secular affairs in such a way as to further God's will. St. Thomas Aquinas a moderate papalist. He preached the view that in secular matters the king should enjoy a good deal of independence.[11]

## AN ESTIMATE OF ST. THOMAS AQUINAS

St. Thomas Aquinas will always be remembered as the greatest political thinkers of his times and one of the greatest of all times. He was the pupil of a great scholastic Albert the Great. He brought back to Europe Aristotle's philosophy which had been forgotten. He tried to bring about a synthesis between Aristotle's philosophy and the Christian teachings.

Synthesis and reconciliation are the main features of his thought. EA discover in his philosophy a synthesis between reason and faith, reconciliation between the Church and the state. He is a representative of the middle ages. He is a forerunner of many modern ideas in political science. His views about the functions of government, his classification of laws and above all, his views about completion of reason by revelation will always shine brightly and brilliantly and will enable the students of political science to understand the complicated and complex political problems and to find a true relation between the secular and spiritual aspects of life.[12]

## REFERENCES

1. Foster says, The writers of the period were civil lawyers, canon lawyers, writers on Christian doctrines, commentators on the scriptures, apologies for the Pope, apologies for the emperor. St. Thomas assimilated these elements into the unity of a single system.
2. Sabine says "Faith is the fulfilment of reason. Together, they complete the temple of knowledge, but nowhere they conflict or work at cross-purposes."
3. Quoted by Dunning, p. 196.
4. According to Foster, he was one of the great systematic philosophers of the world. He represents the totality of medieval thought.
5. Dunning says, St. Thomas Aquinas is the greatest of the later scholastics and perhaps of all scholastics.
6. Dunning, A History of political theories, p. 200.
7. Foster says, the function of the temporal ruler is compared with that of the ship's carpenter, whose task is to keep the ship in repair while on voyage. The task of the Church is like that of the pilot, who has to steer the ship to the goal of its voyage.
8. Sabine, A History of Political Theory, p. 251.

   Sabine says, "Thomas Aquinas's constant attempt was to relate human law as closely as possible to divine law."
9. Sabine, A History of Political Theories, *op. cit.*, p. 262.

   He says "It is the eternal plan of divine wisdom by which the whole creation is ordered."
10. Sabine, A History of Political Theory, p. 265.

He says "By divine law, Thomas Aquinas meant substantially revelation".

11. Sabine, *op. cit.,* p. 270-275.

12. St. Thomas Aquinas views about the nature and functions of government, and above all, his classification of law and his views about justice have made him an immortal political thinker.

# 7

# Dante and Padua
## (1265 A.D.—1321 A.D.)

### Introduction

Dante was a great secularist, a great Italian poet, soldier, political theorist, an idealistic lover, a man of affairs, a lyric poet, a painter and a philosopher.[1] He was reared in Florence, educated in classical and medieval texts of rhetoric and theology. Dante was a great Italian patriot. He was a famous poet. He aimed at glorifying Italy. He was a great utopian. He wanted to re-unite Italy. He thought that papal policy was a source of never-ending dissension. In his two greatest works—The De Monarchia and divine comedy demanded a separation of Church and state, a strong emperor as well as a strong Pope. The struggle between spiritual and temporal rules have been disastrous and Dante sought the solution by destroying the rivalry by effecting a clear separation of powers. He had to spend several years in exile and gained considerable experience when he went from city to city and court to court.

### The Background

Dante was born in the 13th century and lived into the 14th. He was a Renaissance in himself. His native city was Florence. It was a center of literacy and artistic activity equalled only by the golden age of Athens. After completing his education, he began his life as a soldier. He had studied Latin poetry, ancient and scholastic philosophy, rhetoric, theology and mathematics. The study of Aristotle had left a deep impact on him and he called him "The master of those who know." From Aristotle, he derived his ethics, metaphysics, and some of his basic principles of his political theory. His family background was middle class. His father belonged to the ancient nobility, not wealthy country landowners but part of the economic life of the commercial and industrial commune, and his grand father was a money lender at Florence and this business was carried on by Dante's father also.

His Monarchia was turbulent. In 1295 he joined one of the powerful Florentile guilds and within five years he had been elected one of the six quild representatives to govern the city. The bitter conflicts between the Black's and White's broke out again Dante and his co-governors refused to help the papal forces. In 1301 Dante was sent to Rome to seek peace. During his absence, the Blacks captured power by a coup and the Pope's full authority over Florence was re-established. In January 1302 Dante was fined, exiled and sentenced to be burnt alive if he is returned to Florence. He was reduced to the position of a wanderer and after getting disillusioned with the character of the Whites, he formed a single party for himself living in temporary asylums granted by the patrons, he went a wandering in the whole of Italy. It was in 1312-15 that he composed the Commedia and De-monarchia. In his childhood (he was 9 years then) he met a girl of his age Beatrice who left the lasting impression on his mind. Even though they met each other just a few times and both were married to others yet when she died in 1290 at the age of 24, she was completely shaken, and nearly went out of his mind.

## DANTES WORKS

### De Monarchia

This book contains the loftiest expression of the Dante's divine scheme of government. In that conception God's government of the universe rests on the principle of unity. For government to be good must be government by one and God is one. Infact, the distinction between the state and the Church in the context of the Middle Ages is misleading for it arose at the time of Reformation. The Middle Ages regarded the human race as a single society administered by two hierarchies of rulers ecclesiastical and temporal and the distinction between the two is one of office, function and jurisdiction.

De Monarchia is divided into three books. In the first book, he defines the nature of the state and the end and functions of the civil authority. The principle formulated that Monarchy alone can ensure human welfare which is the end of the state. Dante, in this part, marshals both speculative and practical argument in support of the claims of monarchical government. In book second, he contends that the best universal state in history has been uninterrupted military successes, rested on divine sanction. In book third, the scheme is that the basis of temporal authority is not the Pope, but it is God and therefore the imperial power in all matters, secular is independent of the papal power. In this way, universe is divided into two categories—one which is attainable in time and the other in eternity with the aid of two guides—The emperor guide to temporal felicity, and the Pope guide to perfect bliss and peace.[2]

### The Law of Comedia

This book seek to depict the progress from grief to joy. Dante at the age of 35 on the evening of the good Friday in 1300 is lost a dark wood from which he wants to move towards a hill illuminated by the sun, but wild beasts a leopard, a lion and a wolf bar his path back to the wood.

His dark wood was a theology. It has political significance. It is interpreted as a state of separation from God, morally an unworthy or evil way of life, but politically it is the anarchy of Dante's Italy. Dante's comedia is that to remove those living in this life from a state of misery and to lead them to a state of happiness. He is thus not a theologian or mere a poet indulging infantasies. Infact, the last chapter of De Monarchia expounds the basic socialism of the Comedia. The sun is the light of love, and the three wild beasts are lust, pride and avarice. The sinners who reside in the hell are damned one's who are incapable of repentance and their tormented existence is hell is a mere continuation of their lives on earth.

The denizens of the purgatory are those who are repenting their sins through suffering. The dark wood is left only with the guidance of Virgil who announces the advent of Christ-celestial paradise is the life of grace and contemplation. Virgil is one guide (like able to the emperor) and Beatrice is a divine force (likeable to the Church). Both are sent to guide Dante out of the darkwood. In this sense, the entire poem is nothing but an allegorical description of Dante's philosophy ethics and political theory. The two guides—the emperor and the Pope willed by providence are missing. But the moral of the poem is that man need not worry. He can still by his unaided powers, if he mediates on his own duties and destiny as an immortal soul, rediscover the straight way of a virtuous life which leads him to perfection. Thus, the empire by controlling greed and lust leads to terrestrial paradise the Church by living a pure and poor life, leads to celestial paradise.

**His Political Ideas**

Dante is the child of his age, he was reflecting the effort of medieval thought to do full justice alike to the claims of the universal whole, and those to the individual.

He argues step by step to show how monarchy alone can achieve the supreme end of the state. He begins by saying that man is different from the rest of the creation in that he does not merely exist, but he has the power of reason or understanding which no other species has. The understanding means speculation. Speculation leads to action. The highest action is to act for peace. Peace must be the universal peace. Universal peace can be best be secured by a universal emperor. The arguments advanced in support of this thesis range from the meta-physical through ethical to pragmatic and historical. The principle of universality or unity is basic to a single man, to the family, to the village, to the city and the kingdom. The ruling principle in every case is one.[3]

Dante expressed his anti-papal views and supported the cause of monarchy in his book De Monarchia. His most famous book is De Monarchia. This book was published in 1311 A.D.

In this book, Dante pleaded that only a world-empire can secure universal peace. He preached that there was perfect peace under the Roman emperors. He upheld the view that imperial authority was derived direct from God. According to Dante, justice and liberty are possible only under world monarchy. Government to be good must be government by one.

He said, the king is the head of the legal system and is subject to law. To Dante, the empire was law personified, law throned and crowned, and invested with majesty and honour. The state is independent of the Church. Dante, the writer of two famous books, De Monarchia and Divine comedy is famous for his views about the relation between the Church and state. He separates the Church and the state and makes the king independent of the pope. Dante is in favour of a strong emperor and a strong Pope. Dante believes that in case of functions of the Pope and the king are separated, they will be able to perform their duties effectively for betterment of mankind.[4]

Dante advocates the view that only a strong monarch can secure universal peace and welfare of the people. The emperor guides man to the blessedness of this life and the Pope guides man to the blessedness of life eternal. According to Dante, reverence to law and authority is most essential. He advocates the view that the traitors to the empire and traitors to the Church deserve punishment. If liberty is to be more than an empty name, it must be founded upon reverence for authority and law.

### An Estimate of Dante

Dante was a great Italian poet, a shining star of thirteenth and fourteenth centuries in the realm of political philosophy. He was a writer of two famous books Divine Monarchia and Divine Comedy. He was a supporter of a world empire, strong monarch and universal peace. He was in favour of separating the Church from the state. He wanted the king and the Pope to be strong in their respective spheres.

## MARSIGLIO OF PADUA
## 1270 A.D.—1340 A.D.

### Introduction

Marsiglio of Padua was the most original thinker of the middle ages.[5] He was colleague of William of Ockam at the University of Paris. He was a secularist and anti-papalist. He opposed the authority of the poem and defended the cause of monarchy in his book De Fensor Pacis (Defender of the peace). According to Gettel, this is the greatest and most original political treatise.

Like St. Thomas Aquinas, Marsiglio of Padua was influenced by Aristotles ideas. But he did not bring about a synthesis between Aristotles philosophy and Christian teachings. He separated ethics from philosophy and ethics from theology. He thought that theology was not essential to enable us to lead a good life.

Marsiglios of Padua was an Averroist. In other words, he was a rationalist and naturalist. According to him, theology contributes nothing to rational knowledge. Happiness is attained in this life without the aid of God. Moral living, according to Aristotle's ethics suffices for salvation. We see a powerful influence of Aristotle's political philosophy on Marsiglio's views about the state and the classification of states.

### Marsiglio's Ideas About the State

Like Aristotle, Marsiglio's of Padua believed that the state is a natural association and is the result of social instinct. He believed that the state is a natural institution and is the result of social instinct. He insisted on self-sufficiency of the state and pointed out that all the classes must work together for the welfare of the people. Marsiglio believed that the state should have everything for its continued existence. To him the community should have the power of legislation. The community can give the power of legislation to its agent. Like Aristotle, Marsiglio was in favour of a small city-state. Marsiglio was of opinion that the state should be self-sufficient to satisfy the physical and moral needs of the people. The state is the highest association for promoting the material and moral welfare of the people.[6]

Marsiglio of Padua gives the same forms of government as Aristotle does. Like Aristotle, Marsiglio says that there are three good types of government in which the rulers rules for the welfare of the people. These good types of government are Monarchy, Aristocracy and Polity. Three bad or diseased types of government in which the rulers rule for their own interest are Tyranny, Oligarchy and Monarchy.

According to Marsiglio, law is supreme in the community. The source of law is the people or a major part of the people. To Marsiglio, God's will is not the source of human law. Human will is the source of human law. Human law is the command of the whole body of people and the violator of law should be punished. According to Marsiglio, coercion is necessary for enforcement of law.

**The Relation Between the State and the Church**

We may mention the following points in Marsiglio's views about the relation between the state and the Church.

**1. The State is Independent of the Church in Secular and Temporal Matters**

Padua was a strong supporter of independence of the state from, the Church. According to him, the Church should be concerned with the spiritual side of the life of the people. It should not interfere at all in the secular and temporal matters. In the secular and temporal matters, the king is totally independent.

**2. The Church is Subordinate to the State**

According to Marsiglio the Church is subordinate to the state in all secular matters. The clergy are subject to laws of the state like laymen. The main duty of the clergy is the celebration of religious rites. They can advise and instruct. They cannot claim exemption from taxes. Marsiglio is of opinion that the clergymen should lead a life of poverty and should not possess more than is necessary for subsistence. The property of the

Church, according to him, belongs to the persons who donated that property to the Church.

**General Council to Govern the Church**

Marsiglio suggests that there should be a Church Council to govern the Church. The final authority of the Church should be in the hands of the Church Council. The clergy and the laymen should be represented in the general council.

**Critical Remarks**

Though, describing the relation between the state and the Church, Marsiglio of Padua strikes a new path, yet there are many shortcomings in his views. Some of his arguments are far from being clear. There are repetitions and contradictions. Same times the main argument is lost in a maze of reasoning. His views about the position of the clergy are not clear. His views about the General Council is not possible.

**Marsiglio's Contributions**

1. Most Original Thinker Marsiglio of Padua was the Most Original Thinker of the Middle Age.
2. Understood the secrets of statesmanship very clearly. The secrets of statesmanship were understood by him very clearly and minutely. In understanding these secrets he surpassed all his contemporaries. He shows a deeper insight into human associations than any other political thinker of medieval age.
3. More modern, than medieval. Though like St. Thomas Aquinas, Marsiglio of Padua is a representative of the middle ages, yet we can find many modern ideas in his political thought. Marsiglio of Padua frees himself from the traditions of the medieval age and shows imagination for the future. He influences the philosophers like Machiavelli, Hooker, Hobbes, Locke, Luther and Montesquieu. He is a link between Medievalism and Modernism. He is not at all bound by the ideas of his times. The vision of the future is clearly present before his secular and imaginative mind.

4. Forerunners of many political philosophies of modern times.

We can read many modern ideas in Marsiglio's philosophy :

(I) The authority of the ruler is dependent on the will of the community.

(II) He is a forerunner of the modern idea of limited monarchy.

(III) He is a forerunner of Hobbes, Benthan and Austin because he points out that coercion is necessary for enforcement of laws.

(IV) He is a forerunner of Renaissance. He points out that happiness of this world is an important as spiritual salvation to be attained in the other world.

(V) He is a forerunner of Montesquieu, the French philosopher who gave theory of separation of powers in his book the 'Spirit of the Laws'

**Conclusion**

A great secularist, a follower of Aristotle, writer of a great treatise, Defensor Pacis (Defender of the peace), which is a landmark in the history of political thought, a pioneer of many modern political ideas, a forerunner of the theory of popular sovereignty, and above all, a political thinker who made the Church subordinate to the state, Marsiglio will be remembered as a link between Medievalism and Modernism.

To him goes the credit of making Political Science independent of theology at a time when the medieval writers were trying to subordinate the state to the Church. He recognized the importance of reason and made a valuable contribution to the theory of law.[7]

## REFERENCES

1. Gettel, History of Political Thought, p. 126.

2. Sabine, A History of Political Theories, pp. 287-288.

3. Dunning, A History of Political Theories, p. 162.
4. Dunning, *op. cit.,* p. 168.
5. Padua is a great secularist, rationalist and a great political thinker of the medieval ages.
6. Like Aristotle Padua believes that state is the association of associations. It's aim is the highest welfare of the people.
7. Sabine, A History of Political Theories, p. 172.

# Bibliography


1. Aron, R.S. : Main Currents in Sociological Thoughts.
2. Barker, Ernest : 1. Greek Political Theories, 2. The Political Thoughts of Plato and Aristotle.
3. Bhandari, D.R : History of European Political Philosophers.
4. Dunning, W.A. : A History of Political Theories.
5. Ebestein : Great Political Thinkers.
6. Foster, M.B. : Master of Political Thought.
7. Gupta, R.C. : Great Political Thinkers.
8. Gupta, M.G. : Western Political Thought.
9. Hearnshaw F.J.C. (Ed.) : The Social and Political Ideas of Some Representative Thinkers of the Revolutionary Era.
10. Johari, R.C. : Political Thoughts.
11. Maxey, C.C. : Political Philosophies.
12. Sabine, G.H. : A History of Political Theory.
13. Sharma, K.N. : Western Political Thought.
14. Sudha, J.P. : History of Political Thought.
15. Waypar, C.L. : Political Thought.

# Index

R